ANT MIDDLETON

FIRST MAN IN

LEADING FROM THE FRONT

SNIPER.
SOLDIER.
SURVIVOR.

HarperCollins*Publishers*

HarperCollins*Publishers*
1 London Bridge Street
London SE1 9GF

www.harpercollins.co.uk

First published by HarperCollins*Publishers* 2018

HB impression 6
TPB impression 3

A catalogue record of this book is
available from the British Library

HB ISBN 978-0-00-824571-9
PB ISBN 978-0-00-824572-6

Printed and bound in Great Britain by
CPI Group (UK) Ltd, Croydon, CR0 4YY

MIX
Paper from
responsible sources
FSC C007454
www.fsc.org

For Emilie

To the only person who can make me or break
me with one sentence. This woman pushes me on
a daily basis and will not accept anything less
than one hundred per cent from me at all times.
When I lose my way, she redirects me. When I put
a foot out of place, she stamps on it. And when I
fail, she is the only person who can lift me back
up and make me feel invincible. My wife is the
reason I am here today and she is the lady
that has made me the man I am.

CONTENTS

CONTENTS

INTRODUCTION

OF ALL THE people that I meet in my day-to-day life, most don't have the courage to ask The Question. The majority only know me from the television and so are aware that I served two tours of Afghanistan with the Special Forces. Because my first TV appearance was on Channel 4's *SAS: Who Dares Wins*, it's often assumed that I was a member of the Special Air Service. In fact, I was a Special Boat Service operator. In military parlance I was a point man. My job was to lead a small group of men into Taliban compounds, searching out high-status targets on dangerous 'hard arrest' missions. Because of the great secrecy that surrounds Special Forces operations, I can't talk about them. But I am able to give you a very general answer to The Question.

Killing someone feels like gently pulling your trigger finger back a few millimetres. It feels like hearing a dull pop. It feels like seeing a man-shaped object fall away from your sights. It feels like getting the job done. It feels satisfying. But, beyond that, killing someone feels like nothing at all. You might find that shocking. You might even find it offensive. I'm aware, of course, that mine is not an ordinary response. It's not even a response that I share with everyone who's fought in war. Many brave men I served alongside will remain forever traumatised by the horrors they've witnessed and taken part in. I truly feel for them. Being part of a 'hard arrest' team meant working regularly in conditions of life-threatening stress and being surrounded, almost every day, by blood and killing. But my struggle wasn't with the trauma all that created. Mine was with its satisfaction. I'd enjoyed it – perhaps, at times, too much. I thrived on combat. I still miss it every day.

In Afghanistan, getting shot at was a regular occurrence. You came to expect it. I viewed survival as a numbers game. As point man, every time I entered a Taliban compound or a room within a compound and knew that there was badness on the other side, I played the odds in my head. It was a bit like roulette – a calculated risk. I'd think, 'What are the chances of me going through that door and there's a combatant there who knows I'm coming? If they do know I'm coming, what are the chances of them being able to fire more than one bullet before I shoot at them? What are the chances that one bullet's going to hit me in the head and kill me?' When I thought of it like that, I'd usually come to realise the chances were pretty slim. So I'd think, 'Fuck it, the odds are with me,' and that would get me through the door.

Sometimes, at this point of entry, there'd be bullets flying in my direction. But experience told me these bursts were usually over in seconds and that the moment there was a pause in firing I could make my move – entering crouched low, because idiots with AKs usually can't control the natural lift of their weapons and they spray rounds at the ceiling when they fire. I'd think, 'If he pulls the trigger again, he'll only have the chance to squeeze it once or twice, max, before I get the drop on him.' If one or two rounds did come out of his weapon and strike me in the chest plate, it would only be my chest plate. If they hit me in the leg, they'd only immobilise me for a split second. If I fell down, I knew my pal would be right behind me, on my shoulder, and would finish the job in a blink. That was how I saw it – a numbers game. Always the odds. Always a little calculation in my head.

Which is not to say I found it easy. Far from it. Going into an operation, the fear would be horrendous. But as soon as it all began – the moment I breached the compound or made contact with the enemy – I'd enter a completely different psychological space. The only thing I can compare it to is the final seconds before a car smash, when you see how it's all going to play out in slow motion. Your brain goes into a hyper-efficient state, absorbing so much information from your surroundings that it really does feel as if the clock has suddenly slowed down – as if you've got the ability to control time itself.

This enabled me to act with a level of precision in which it seemed I could count in milliseconds. It was a state of pure focus, pure action, pure instinct, every cell in my body working in perfect harmony with each other towards the same end, at a level of peak performance. I didn't feel any emotion. There was only awareness, control and action. It was the closest thing I could imagine to feeling all-powerful, like God. And that's what I was, in a way. When I was point man in the middle of a dangerous operation, godlike was how my mind and body felt – and godlike was how I had to act in judging, in a fraction of an instant, who lived and who died.

The first man I ever killed came out at me from the hot, dusty shadows of an Afghan compound. It was night. He was wearing a traditional white ankle-length robe, called a dish-dash. There was a thick strap over his right shoulder. In his hands, an AK-47. He stopped, then squinted into the darkness. He couldn't see me. He stared some more. His neck craned forwards. He saw the two green eyes of my night-vision goggles staring back at him from the blackness. And then it came, an event I'd soon know well. While a lot goes on within it, the moment of death always has an order, a sure sequence of events. It happens like this: Shock. Doubt. Disbelief. Confusion. Your target feels an urge to double-check a situation that they can't quite believe is happening. Their thoughts race. Their lips open just a few millimetres. Their eyes squint into the night. Their chin moves forward. Their body begins to change its stance. And then ...

That moment – the one I'd watch happening time after time after time in Afghanistan in intimate, ultra-slow motion – is our secret weapon. Staying alive, and achieving our objective, relied on tiny fractions of time such as this. Special Forces soldiers are trained to operate between the tremors of the clock's ticking hand, slipping in and out and doing their work in the time it takes for the enemy to turn one thought into another. And that's how it went the night of my first kill. From my position in the corner of the compound I took half a step forwards, raised my weapon and squeezed the trigger once, then twice. The suppressor I'd screwed to the barrel made the firing of the bullets sound like little more than the clicks of a computer mouse. Perfect shots. Two in the mouth. He went down.

The Special Forces are looking for individuals who have the ability to do this as a job, day in, day out, and not let it destroy them. That was me. People like this aren't born this way. They're made. This book is not just lessons in leadership that I've learned over the years. It's the story of how I became the man I am. It's a tale of a naive and gentle young lad whose first memory is of his beloved father being found dead. It's the tale of struggle and pain and fury in the army, of darkness and violence on the streets of Essex, of days in war zones, days in prison, days hunting down kidnapped girls in foreign lands, days leading men out of impossible hells. It's the story of how I became the kind of individual who leads from the front and who, no matter what danger he's charging into, always wants to be first man in.

STRANGE NOISES. PEOPLE moving about. People talking. Footsteps. Heavy, grown-up footsteps that I didn't recognise. I sat up in bed and tried to wake myself by squeezing and rubbing my eyes with the backs of my hands. It was the week after Christmas – perhaps Mum and Dad were having a party. I climbed down from my top bunk past my brother's bed, which was empty. On the chest of drawers there was my favourite toy, a plastic army helicopter that Dad had bought for my fifth birthday. I reached up on tiptoes and gave its black propellers a push. I was about to take it down when I heard someone crying. I turned towards the sound. Through the crack in the door I saw a policeman.

I slipped out and followed him, barefoot in my grey pyjamas, in the direction of my parents' bedroom. I passed two more policemen in the corridor who were talking and didn't seem to notice me. Lights were blazing in my mum and dad's room. There were even more policemen in there, four, maybe five of them, crowded around the bed. Intrigued and excited, I pushed between the legs of two of them and peered up to see what they were all looking at. There was someone under the sheets. Whoever it was, they weren't moving. I shuffled forward for a better view.

'No! No! No!' a policeman shouted. He bent down and manoeuvred me back down the corridor into the other bedroom, his bony fingertips pressing into my shoulders. My brothers were all in there, Peter, Michael and Daniel. Someone had taken the television up there from downstairs. They were all watching it. I sat down in the corner. I didn't say a word.

My next memory is about four weeks later. I was being woken up again: 'Anthony! Anthony! Come on, Anthony. Wake up.' The main light was on. There were two people standing over me, my mum and this man I'd never seen before. He was enormously tall, with a big nose and long, dark hair that went down past his shoulders. I didn't know how old he was, but I could see he was much younger than Mum.

'Anthony,' she said. 'Meet your new dad.'

DON'T LET ANYONE DEFINE WHO YOU ARE

IT FELT AS if we'd been driving for days. I gazed out of the car window, watching motorways turn to A-roads turn to winding, hedge-crowded country lanes, with every mile we travelled bringing me closer and closer to the new life I'd chosen for myself and further away from the familiarity of the family home and everything I loved, hated and feared. The clouds hung above us like oily rags and the November wind battered on the roof of our Ford Sierra as it sputtered through the Surrey countryside. Neither me, my mum nor my stepfather spoke much. We let the English weather do the talking for us. As the wheels of the car pounded the tarmac, anxious thoughts span around my head. Had I made the right decision? Would I find myself and thrive in my new home? Or was I just swapping one unpredictable hellhole for another? Who was I going to be when this new journey ended? If I'd known the answer to that, I'd have opened the car door and jumped straight out.

The truth was, back in 1997 I didn't have much of an idea who I was as a person. Who does when they're seventeen?

At that age we like to think we're fully defined human beings, but the fact is we're barely out of life's starting blocks. We've spent our childhood being defined by teachers, parents, brothers, sisters, tinpot celebrities on the TV and, in the middle of all that, is a squishy lump of dough who's constantly being shaped and reshaped. That's why, especially when we're young, it's crucial that we're surrounded by people whose influence is going to be positive and who are interested in building up our strengths, rather than drowning us in our weaknesses. I know that now. I wish I'd known it then.

Eventually, on the side of a narrow road, a red sign came into view. I couldn't read what it said through the steam and raindrops on my window, so I rubbed the condensation away with the sleeve of my sweatshirt. MILITARY ROAD: ALL VEHICLES ARE LIABLE TO BE STOPPED. I sat up and took a deep breath. The car slowed down. There was another sign, a white notice that just said PIRBRIGHT CAMP. Beyond that was a guard room outside tall, black gates. And then, the sign I had been looking for: NEW RECRUITS REPORT HERE. 'Here we go, Mum,' I said, trying to disguise the nervousness in my voice. 'This is it.'

She pulled up in a lay-by. I got out, lifted my heavy black bag from the boot and gave her a quick kiss on the cheek. If she was sad to see me go, she did a good job of hiding it. My stepfather wound his window down, gave me the thumbs-up and said, 'Good luck. See you later,' then looked away.

Before I had the chance to think, Mum was back in the car, closing her door and turning her key in the ignition. The engine fired up and I watched them vanish into the grey-green scenery. I took a moment to steady myself. This was it. From now on, everything was going to be different.

I took a deep breath, picked up my bag, slung it over my shoulder and turned towards the domineering complex of red-brick buildings. It looked like a prison or maybe a large hospital. There were rolls of barbed wire on the tops of the walls and security cameras on tall poles facing this way and that. I couldn't see anyone else or hear any voices. I felt completely alone. It was almost creepy.

I approached the guard room nervously, almost expecting there to be nobody behind the glass window. When I was two steps away it was pulled open with a crack and a skinny guy in his mid-twenties, wearing military greens and those round John Lennon-style glasses, peered out. I flashed him my best friendly, charming and disarming smile. 'I'm reporting for Basic Training, sir,' I told him.

The soldier gave me a look like a bird had crapped on his spectacles.

'Sir? Don't call me Sir. I work for a living. It's "Corporal" to you. Name?'

'Middleton, Corporal,' I said. 'Royal Engineers.'

He picked up a clipboard that had been lying on his desk and scanned it lazily. 'Middleton … Middleton … Middleton …'

I shifted my bag onto my other shoulder and tried to squeeze some blood back into my hand. He turned the sheet over and carried on running his fingertip down it. Then, very slowly, he reached over, picked up a second clipboard and began examining that one instead. The winter wind whipped around my neck. Finally, his finger stopped.

'Ah,' he said. 'Anthony. Is that it? Anthony Middleton?'

'Yes, Corporal.'

He smiled at me warmly. 'Found you!'

I felt a huge rush of relief. Maybe this wasn't going to be so bad after all.

'You're not due until next week,' he said. And with that, his window slammed shut with another loud crack.

I was so stunned that all I could do was stand there, gazing at my reflection. Looking back at me in the glass I saw an immaculately presented, naive, skinny teenager with blue eyes and thick black eyebrows that met in the middle. A nice young lad with not a clue what to do. I walked back into the road with my head down but could only go so far before I had to put my bag down again.

What was I going to do? How the hell had I got the date wrong? I couldn't believe it. My mum and stepdad would be a couple of miles away by now. I scanned the muddy landscape in the vague hope I might spot a telephone box so I could call someone. There were trees bare of leaves, some far-off horses in a field and a flock of anonymous birds careening in the distance. There was no telephone box. And who would I call anyway? Where could I sleep? I had no sleeping bag, nor enough money for a B&B. Maybe I could find a dry spot out of the way by the barracks wall. How was I going to last a week in the wet with no food? How could I begin my British Army basic training course starving, soaking and probably ill?

I had a sudden, almost overwhelming urge to get as far away from the army buildings as quickly as possible. Instead, I put my head down, gritted my jaw and paced up the road, back towards those imposing black gates. I'd have to find somewhere to camp out in the dry and my best bet, I thought, was to use some of that man-made infrastructure. Once I was settled somewhere I'd come up with a plan. I tried to think positively. There must be a town not far away. I could find a call box there and get hold of Mum. I wasn't sure whether she'd come and get me, to be honest, but towns mean homeless people, and homeless people have shelters and maybe I could …

'Oi!' came a shout. 'Where you going, mate?'

I stopped and turned. On my way I'd passed a smaller brick guard hut. It hadn't looked occupied but a man in army fatigues was now hanging out of the door, barking at me.

'You can't go up there, mate.'

I stopped and turned back.

'This is a military area,' he said. 'What you doing here? Who are you?'

'I'm afraid I've got my dates wrong,' I told him with an embarrassed shrug. 'I have to come back next week, so ...' I smiled, as if the whole thing was no bother at all.

'New recruit?' he said.

'Yes.'

He shook his head and pointed with his chin back towards the large guard house. 'Get over there and knock on his window,' he said. 'He's fucking with you.'

Half an hour later I found myself standing in a large, spotless room in a line-up of new recruits. We'd come from across the length and breadth of the British Isles in all shapes and sizes, young, spotty, greasy and hairy, none of us comfortable in our own skin and yet all of us desperately acting like we were. A corporal was walking up and down the lines of bodies, silently examining us with an unimpressed eye. The sound of his clicking heels echoed around the shining walls and polished floors. He seemed to tower over us, his spine erect, his broad shoulders filling out his shirt so that the khaki material stretched tightly against his skin. I tried to stop my eyes following him around the room but it was impossible. As he approached closer and closer to me, I forced them forwards and raised my chin just a little bit higher and puffed out my skinny chest as far as I could. The corporal stopped. He stopped right in front of me. My eyes widened. My heart froze.

'Name?' he said.

'Middleton, Corporal.'

He turned and bent down so that his face was barely an inch from mine.

'Middleton,' he growled. 'In the British Army we prefer our men to have two eyebrows.'

'Yes, Corporal.'

He walked on. My eyes didn't follow. My cheeks burned. I was intimidated, I was disorientated and was wondering what the hell I'd got myself into.

After some brief words from the corporal, we were sent to our accommodation block to settle in. We were shown into a big room with a gleaming parquet wooden floor. There were rows and rows of identical beds with itchy blankets, and wooden lockers with their doors hanging open. Everything in there was immaculate. Spotless. For the first time I felt almost at home: this was exactly how my step-father had always forced us to keep house. I found myself a bed – a bottom bunk in a far corner of the block – and took the opportunity to have a scan of all the others. There must have been about thirty lads in there, some teenagers like me, others in their early twenties. I guessed it probably wasn't a coincidence that I'd been highlighted, like that, by the corporal. I looked different from the others. I wasn't like them. You could just tell.

*　*　*

THE TRUTH IS, most of the young men who'd turned up for Basic Training that day were tough working-class lads who'd grown up immersed in the British culture of drinking, bantering and bashing the shit out of each other.

My childhood hadn't been anything like that. After my dad had died completely unexpectedly on 31 December 1985, my mother and stepfather had suddenly come into a lot of money. There was some confusion over my dad's true cause of death, but it was eventually ruled that he'd had a heart attack. This official verdict meant his life insurance could pay out. My mum and her new boyfriend Dean, who'd been around from almost the precise moment my dad passed away, were suddenly awash with money. The family moved from a three-bed house in Portsmouth to an eight-bed mansion outside Southampton.

Suddenly, everything was different. Me and my brothers were decked out in designer clothes, driven about in expensive cars and educated in the better private schools. My mum really started spoiling us. One Christmas it took us about three days to open all our presents. Then, when I was nine, the whole family upped and moved to northern France. We had a large, rambling plot of land with a big house that was once a farm on the outskirts of a town called Saint-Lô, twenty miles from Bayeux. I attended a well-respected Catholic school and was always neatly presented, and extremely polite and respectful. Almost overly so. People would love it when I came to their house because they knew the dishes would get done. I was a product of that much more gentle and civilised French culture.

I'd experienced my first hint of difference between the two nations on a visit back to the UK to see my maternal grandparents. There'd been a guy about the same age as me walking down the street, strutting along, and he just started staring at me. In French culture, you tip your hat, you're polite and respectful. When you pass someone in the street you say 'Bonjour' and 'Ça va?' So I said, 'All right?' He just glared at me like he wanted to kill me. I didn't realise he was doing that stupid young-lad thing of who can stare the other one out. I found it so strange. I just thought, 'What a weirdo.'

I couldn't have been more different from these people. I'd grown up in a place where fourteen-year-olds visit bars to drink coffee, not to down jugs of vodka Red Bull until they beat each other senseless, then puke.

I OPENED MY bag, commandeered a locker and squared away all my kit, folding it neatly and piling it up. And then, as quickly as I could, I took my wash-bag and a disposable Bic razor to the toilet block. I popped the orange cap off the blade and held it under cold water, then, with a firm hand, I placed it on the base of my forehead and pulled it down over the black fuzz that connected my eyebrows. As I bent down to rinse the blade under the tap, I heard the voice of the corporal echoing out of the nearby dormitory. 'Right, get your fucking PT kit on, you lot,' he barked. 'I want you lined up out on the parade ground in sixty seconds.'

I glanced up at the mirror to examine my handiwork. I couldn't believe it. I'd shaved off a wide rectangle of hair, the precise length of the razor, from above my eyes. The good news – I had two eyebrows. The bad news – I looked like I'd been run over by a tiny lawnmower. 'Fuck,' I muttered. I ran back into the dorm, dodging the squints and smirks, and got changed as quickly as possible into the physical training kit that had been left out for us, folded perfectly at the end of each narrow bed.

Out in the parade square we lined up in three rows in our green T-shirts and blue shorts. All I could do was pray the corporal didn't spot what I'd done to my face and decide to humiliate me all over again. He took his place in front of us on the tarmac and stood legs apart, his hands behind his back.

'I've got bad news for you lot,' he said, scanning the lines of faces, each of which was trying hard not to show the cold, jaws clamped, nostrils flaring. 'There's been a minor cock-up. We've got too many of you here. We don't have enough places. Not enough beds. "What does that mean?" I hear you ask. What it means is that some of you are going to have to stand back for two weeks and join the next intake.'

Was he being serious? Was this another wind-up? It was impossible to know.

'So how are we going to choose between you?' he continued. 'How are we going to make this fair? We're going to kick off this morning with a Basic Fitness test. We'll begin with a mile-and-a-half run. You'll have to complete that mile-and-a-half run in ten minutes or less, gentlemen. You'll be competing. This will be a race. And the prize for the winner, and only the winner, is one guaranteed bed.'

With that we were marched off the parade ground and through the maze of gloomy brick buildings until we reached an airfield on the edge of the base. As soon as we were shown the starting line we began jostling for position. I already had a good sense of where I stood in this pecking order. I didn't have much chance of beating some of these older, bigger, fitter lads. But I told myself I had to at least get into the front half of the pack.

Still jostling – elbows poking, shoulders barging, feet inching forwards – we watched the instructor take his stopwatch in one hand and a steel whistle in the other. The moment I heard that whistle scream, I pushed my way forwards in the pack as best as I could and launched into it with everything I had. I could feel the warmth of the bodies around me, hear the sound of pounding feet and the breathing, feel the muddy turf slip and yield beneath my boots. I pushed harder and harder, desperate to clear the mass, shoving this way and that, finding little routes through the bodies.

By the time I was halfway round the airfield I realised with a shock that there were only two men left in front of me. The sight of all the beautiful clear space in front of us spurred me on. I could feel myself surging with that angry competitive drive my stepfather had always instilled in me. I could practically see him there at the side of the field, with his big leather trench coat and his Rottweiler, shouting at me, telling me I wasn't giving it enough, that I needed to push harder. I'd fucking show him. I picked the first man off and left him comfortably behind, as spots of cold mud flecked my legs and heat burned in my knees. Two hundred metres to go. I took the last bend, my legs pounding. The last man and I were neck and neck, sprinting with everything we had. From out of nowhere I was hit with a flash of the humiliation I'd felt earlier. I imagined my competitor laughing at me. A furious thought entered my head: these bastards think I'm nothing. They think I'm some skinny, mono-browed, nice middle-class boy. I found myself surging forward, faster and faster. By the time I got to the finish line I was a full twelve seconds in front of him. I couldn't believe it. I'd won.

Following that race, I charged with everything I had into this brutal, confusing and sometimes thrilling new world. Every day of Basic Training that followed was painful. We'd have press-ups, sit-ups, pull-ups, assault courses, cross-country running with heavy bergens on our back. With all that and the fieldcraft lessons, we'd hardly a minute to ourselves, and any minutes we did have were spent ironing our kit or making sure our lockers were immaculate. During our first proper inspection, I was waiting by mine and the corporal stopped in front of the lad next to me, a nineteen-year-old called Ivan.

'You look like a bag of shit,' he shouted at him. 'Look at your fucking boots.' As Ivan looked down to see what he was talking about, the corporal punched him in the chest and sent him crashing through his locker, right through the wood at the back, which snapped in half. Ivan lay there, gasping like a fish, in a nest of splinters and dust. One thing I knew for sure: I wasn't in Saint-Lô anymore. I was going to have to toughen up.

At that time I'd only ever thrown one punch in my life, and that was only because the situation had been forced upon me. It had all happened when I was living with my mum and stepdad in Southampton, shortly before my family had left for France. I'd been having some problems with a bully, a guy a couple of years older than me who'd taken it upon himself to make my life as miserable as possible, tripping me up, throwing me against walls and just generally being dumb and menacing. I tried to avoid him as much as possible, but it inevitably started getting me down, to the extent that I didn't want to go into school anymore. When my stepfather noticed something was wrong, I made the mistake of telling him the details.

'Well, what are you doing about it?' he asked.

'Nothing,' I shrugged.

'Do the teachers know? Have you told them?'

'Of course not.'

'Anthony,' he said, 'listen to me. I do not want you to come back to this house until you've punched that boy square in the face. If you don't do that, do not come home tomorrow.'

I couldn't believe what he was saying. I didn't even know how to throw a punch.

'I can't do that,' I said, trying to reverse out of the living room and escape upstairs to my room. 'It doesn't matter.'

'I'm not fucking about, Anthony,' he said, barring my way. 'Until you've properly hurt him, don't even think about coming through this door again.'

The next time I came across the bully he was waiting in the dinner queue. I saw him before he saw me. He was holding a tray with a bowl of chips covered in steaming hot beans and a carton of Ribena on it. He was with his mates, I was alone. Despite the fact that I had no backup, I decided it was then or never. I walked up to him.

'I just want to put everything to bed,' I said. 'Is that all right? Do you want to shake hands?'

The bully just stood there, looking at me, dumb as an ox. To be fair, he was probably trying to work out how he was supposed to shake my hand when he was holding his tray. But whatever it was that was going through his head, I decided that that was my moment. I punched him square in the bridge of the nose. He fell back, chips and beans flying everywhere, cutlery and tray clattering to the ground.

I didn't hang around to see what damage I'd done. I was gone.

Later that afternoon my stepfather received a phone call from the headmaster.

'I'm calling with unfortunate news,' he said. 'I'm afraid I've had to take the difficult decision to suspend Anthony from school for a period of one week.'

'Suspend him?' said my stepfather.

'I'm very sorry to have to let you know that Anthony physically assaulted another pupil today. We can't let something like that pass without taking appropriate steps.'

'Good,' he said. 'I'm glad to hear it.'

'Well, yes, you obviously understand then that even though this was very out of character for Anthony, we do have to ...'

'No, no, no,' he interrupted. 'I'm not saying I'm glad you suspended him. I'm saying I'm glad he hit that prick. I told him to do it. How long did you say he was suspended for?'

'A week.'

'You'll see him in two.'

I can't deny there was a certain pleasure in seeing my tormentor caught under a scalding orange rainstorm of Heinz's finest, though to be honest I wasn't especially proud of myself for hitting back. It might have largely ended my problems with that particular bully, but it just didn't feel like who I was. I did at least manage to take one crucial bit of positivity out of it. From then on I knew I had that capacity within me. When push came to shove, I learned that I could react with some level of violence and cause a bit of damage. But that wasn't the only thing I learned. Over the two-week holiday from school that the punch had earned me, I played the scene over and over in my head. I'd obviously been scared before the moment I struck out, but what exactly had been the source of all that fear? What had been holding me back from sorting the problem out for so long?

I realised it was a dread of the unknown. I was scared of punching the bully because I didn't know what was going to happen next. He could have thrown hot food in my face. His mates could have piled on top of me and kicked me shitless. He could have barely flinched, calmly placed his tray to one side and then calmly broken my jaw. Anything could have happened. That, I realised, was the truth about most of the fear we'll experience in our lives. Humans don't like being in the dark about things. We hate not knowing what's behind the door. We like to be able to see the future, to put one foot in front of the other and walk through life steadily, carefully and predictably.

Learning to cope with deep states of doubt would be the journey of my life in the military. That's one of the things it teaches you – and it's a long, tough lesson, because it's going completely against the grain of your human nature. It was only years later, going into war zones as an operator, that I truly learned to cope with the fear of stepping into unpredictable situations. By that stage I knew that if I got to my target, I could act. I could punch through an enemy position, I could cope with being shot at and, if I needed to, I could pull that trigger and end a life. I had that capacity in me. And the seed of that capacity was planted way back when I was a boy, at that moment in the dinner queue.

When I was a new recruit at Pirbright, those lessons were still an extremely long way off. Three weeks after I'd seen that young lad being posted through a plywood wall, I found myself on the parade ground beside him. We were in formation, waiting for the corporal to arrive for inspection. Next to us, looking confused and out of place, was a new recruit called Neil. He'd joined our troop after falling out of Basic Training, having suffered a broken ankle on week five of his intake. Now he was mostly better, he'd been inserted back into the programme. Neil was a big, leery lad and slightly chubby round the middle, probably out of shape after being out of action for a while.

The problem was that Neil threw the numbers out. We were supposed to be arranged in rows of three, but now we had an odd number of bodies, so there was a gap at the front of our formation. I knew that in this eventuality you were supposed to arrange yourself in such a way that you still looked orderly from the front. The corporal was probably seconds away from rocking up and Neil was in the wrong place. He had to sort himself out, otherwise we'd all be in the shit. I flashed him a friendly smile.

'Mate,' I said to him. 'Why don't you jump up here, because the instructor's going to come any second?'

'Who the fuck are you?' he said, taking a step towards me.

Seeing what was about to happen, Ivan spoke up. 'All right, mate, he's only trying to help you out.'

'And what's your fucking problem?' said Neil.

'You're the one with the fucking problem.'

'Do you want to sort this out then?'

'All right.'

'Once we've knocked off tonight, I'll see you behind building 2D.'

I couldn't understand it. Why was Neil being such a dick? Did he feel, coming into a new troop, that he had to dominate people to get respect? Maybe it was that he'd clocked up a few weeks' more experience than us prior to his injury, and so when I told him where to stand he felt insulted. What was the point of reacting like that? I'd been polite and respectful to him. If I'd have said the same thing in France, I'd have been thanked. But the UK was a completely different culture and these kinds of situations would probably be solved with aggression or outright violence.

'It's dog-eat-dog over here', I thought to myself. 'It really is every man for himself.' The cheeky and helpful manner that people found so charming at my mixed-sex French school were getting me nowhere quickly in this hardcore male-only environment. Rather than it winning me friends and allies, as it had over there, I was being met with an attitude of 'Who the fuck does this prick think he is?' I sensed there was something else going on too. People were defining me by my appearance and my polite cheerfulness. Neil, for one, had seen I wasn't a big lad and was reacting to that, judging me as beneath him. 'You little gobshite,' he seemed to be saying. 'I'm not taking orders from you.'

There was only one thing I could do. Everyone thought I was a soft lad, so I had to prove them wrong. I knew there was going to be a confrontation that night, and given the size differential between Neil and Ivan, my new pal was going to get pasted. As the dark silhouette of the corporal marched towards us, I silently decided I'd join him in the fight. I'd defend him as he'd defended me.

That day passed slowly. When the time came and I saw Ivan slip out of the accommodation block, I trotted after him down the dark path.

'What you doing?' he said.

'You were sticking up for me,' I explained. 'I'm part of this.'

'This is nothing to do with you,' said Ivan.

'I've got to stand up to this guy,' I said. 'I'm going to help you out, aren't I? Otherwise, who am I?'

I liked the way that sounded. Loyal. Tough. But Ivan just laughed in my face.

'It's just not you, Ant, is it?' he said. 'I'm not being funny, mate, but go on. Get back there and get your tea down you before it gets cold.'

I was furious. All my anxieties about what the others thought of me had been summed up in that one dismissive comment. Maybe it was Ivan I should be fronting up to, not Neil.

'How do you fucking know it's not me?' I said.

'Because you're better than that.'

Now that really did hit me, harder than any punch I might be about to take behind the kitchen block. The thing was, I could tell he meant it too. And he was right. What was I doing? Trying to prove I was one of them by turning myself into someone I wasn't? If they thought I was a soft lad, that was their problem. By trying to prove myself to them, I realised, I was actually submitting to them. I was letting them control me. But what was I going to do now? I could hardly leave Ivan to take a beating. I had to ask myself who I was. I was someone, I hoped, who was a bit smarter than the average green army recruit. I was someone who wasn't going to let ego and temper ruin my career. I realised that the only way to deal with this while remaining true to myself was to try to prevent the fight from happening at all.

'Why do you need to fight this guy anyway?' I said.

'You don't get it, Ant,' he said. 'It's not like it is where you come from. It's alpha male. It's who's got the biggest dick. You've got to step up to the plate.'

'We've just joined the army a few weeks ago,' I said. 'If word of this gets out or you tip up to parade with a black eye or a broken nose, they're going to know what's gone on.'

Ivan said nothing.

'You're risking your entire career to prove something to this idiot,' I continued. 'That's not very smart. Do you really care about what he thinks of you that much that you'll put everything on the line?'

He still said nothing.

'You're going to lose your career. You're sacrificing everything you've worked for, for Neil Porlock. You're letting him win, just by turning up.'

After that, it didn't take long to grind him down. He stopped, turned around, and instead of a fight, we went and had a cup of tea and a biscuit.

I CAN'T HELP but look back on that incident with a bit of pride. Even at that young age, and in that tough environment, I was able to keep a grip on who I really was and sense that the alpha-male bully-boy culture was trying to mould me into someone else. Unfortunately, I can't tell you that I managed to maintain that strength of character. As you'll soon discover, I eventually let the worst of the army get the better of me. I became someone who couldn't have been further removed from that polite and gentle young lad.

It never ends, though. People always want to define you. Because these days I'm best known for the Channel 4 show *SAS: Who Dares Wins*, strangers try to define me all the time. They assume I'm this chippy rogue who deals with everything through violence. When they meet me, they expect me to have some hard, judgemental persona. I get people approaching me in the street and talking about my size. They imagine that I'm six foot eight, not five foot eight, and I always get, 'You look bigger on TV.' Or they say, 'I don't know what everyone's so worried about, I reckon I could have it with you.'

They're joking around when they come out with stuff like that … but also they're not. Otherwise, why would they say it? I just laugh it off. I've got nothing to prove. I'm in competition with no one, especially now I'm in the TV world. I mean, it's not as if I feel the need to compete with someone like Bear Grylls, is it? So I banter back with them. 'Yeah, mate, you probably could have me. Don't listen to all that TV stuff. They've got special lenses on their cameras that make me look bigger.' I'm happy to do that. I don't feel threatened at all. I know who I am.

But being an approachable guy doesn't mean I'm a pushover. When I work, I work. I think it's important not to mix business with pleasure. When there's a job to get done, I want to get it done and to the best of my ability. And I want to do it my way. This might sound arrogant, but in my field I genuinely believe that I'm the best at what I do. So while I think it's important to listen to others and not surround myself with Yes men, at the end of the day I'm the leader. I'll make sure the job's done properly, the way I want it done and to my standards. And I expect everyone else to be in that mindset. People know, when they work with me, that they need to snap into a different mode. There's no messing about.

But then when I'm not working I'm a loving father and husband, and I like to think I'm a relaxed guy to be around. That no-nonsense persona is completely gone. It's like I'm two different people. That's why I think it's crucial that you don't define yourself as just one person. That, to me, is the sign of a fake. It's the sign of someone who has this fantasy model of who they want everyone to think they are and just tries to act up to it all the time. When you're true to yourself you know that you're a different person in different situations, and you're totally relaxed about it.

I believe you can only get so far by trying to put on a persona. People who do that always hit a ceiling. They find themselves thinking, 'Right, I've got this far, now who do I have to be to get to this next stage?' If you're yourself, that won't happen. You'll find your own place. You'll get the job done the way you want it done. If you try to be someone else, you'll get lost, because the person who's got you to where you are is a total stranger. He's a fantasy. You don't know who he is. So when new challenges arrive, you'll have to suddenly come up with a different game plan, a different strategy, a different person to be. And that's not a sustainable pattern.

If you're yourself, you'll get to where you're going on your own instincts. There'll be no need to constantly second-guess yourself, thinking, 'Who do I have to be in this moment? How do I have to act? What do I have to say?' You'll be constantly rebooting yourself from scratch. You won't be growing and learning, you'll be panicking. You won't be giving yourself the chance to optimise. When you start on the first square of the grid of being yourself, with every new square you strive to get to you improve who you are. Every struggle you go through will make you a better player. That's what growth is. That's what life's journey is all about. It's about taking who you are and making you a better version of yourself. It's not about trying to be this person or that person. It's not about trying to be like Neil or Ivan. It's not about letting other people define who you are.

This is why I always tell people, don't try to better your life, don't try to better your work, don't try to better your relationships. Don't try to be rich, happy, successful. Don't do any of that. You'll be wasting your time. It doesn't work. Nothing will change, and you'll get disillusioned and burned out. Instead, you should work at trying to better who you are as a character. Be the best version of you that you can imagine, and I guarantee that all the rest of it will just fall naturally into place. Why? Because you're arming yourself. You're giving yourself the tools to be honest with yourself and therefore to be honest with other people. If someone in your life has messed up, you're not going to sit there being too nervous to talk to them about it.

What's not honest is always trying to be the person other people either want you to be or think that you are already. Back in Basic Training, because of the way I looked and spoke, everyone thought I was weak. I could have let that influence me and become weak. For a while I fought against it. There are always going to be people who want to define you by your worst qualities. They pick up on your flaws, zoom in on your most embarrassing and shameful mistakes, and decide that, deep down, that's the person you really are. What makes this especially dangerous is that it's so easy to believe. The trick is not to deny what these negative people are saying. If you do that, you'll look dishonest and inauthentic, and you'll lose the respect of anyone who does admire you. The best response is to accept what they're saying, but know it's only a small part of the truth. Everyone has flaws. Just be up-front about them.

Here's a scenario you might find it useful to think about. Imagine that your particular weakness is physical fitness. Someone has told you that you need to run five miles with a sixty-pound backpack on. If you were to turn around and say, 'Yeah, yeah, no worries at all,' nothing good's going to happen. But what about if you said, 'Actually, I'm going to struggle with that. Physical fitness is not my strong point. I will do it, I'll get the job done, but I need to let you know this is going to be a bit hard for me. I might need a push along the way'? When you're honest like that, I promise you that magical things will happen. People will think, 'This

guy's comfortable with himself. He's not trying to be someone he's not. He's a person who is steadfastly defining
himself. He's an honest person.' And they'll naturally want
to help you out. They'll want to say, 'Do you know what,
mate? I'll give you a hand.'

People don't get annoyed so much when you struggle, but
when you fake it, that's when their walls come up. They get
defensive. Then you're in conflict with that other person.
There's friction and the job is not getting done. People think,
'If I admit my weaknesses, others will have less respect for
me.' But it's actually the other way around.

But there's an exception to all this. Sometimes it's a good
idea to let someone else define who you are. There are times
in your life when someone will see something positive in you
that you didn't realise was there. This is exactly what
happened to me when, at the age of twenty-four, I was going
through Royal Marines training. I'd got to week fifteen of
the thirty-two-week course, at which point a new officer
came in at the top of the hierarchy. He was an older boy, and
everyone respected him. He'd only been there for a couple
of weeks when he summoned me unexpectedly to his office.
I couldn't imagine what he wanted: I was coming first in
everything and keeping myself to myself, so there was no
personal trouble with anyone else, at least that I knew about.

'Middleton,' he said, 'you're in danger of losing grip.'
Losing grip? No I wasn't. I took a moment to make sure my
face wasn't betraying my irritated confusion. 'I'm not quite

sure what the problem is,' he said. 'Perhaps you're getting a bit too big for your boots or perhaps it's just that you're thinking about yourself too much. Well, whatever it is, I'm coming to the conclusion very rapidly that you're not a team man. You need to understand something that's crucially important if you want to achieve your full potential in this organisation. The Royal Marines aren't here to provide you with a pyramid to stand on top of. You, Middleton, are a part of that pyramid. You're just another brick. Do you understand what I'm getting at?'

'I think so, sir,' I said.

'You don't have to prove that you're the best. That's not what all this is about. I think you have a lot more to offer than merely being number one. You've got to think about the bigger picture. You might be leading all the scoreboards but you're not actually *leading*. The kind of men we prize here are the ones who bring the others with them. I think you have that in you.'

There was absolutely nothing I could say. He was right. All I wanted was to be the best at PT, the best at exercise, the first man at map-reading, and so on. I used to study alone. If tests were coming up about fieldcraft or map-reading I'd be in my corner, getting my head down, making it clear that no one should disturb me. I'd assumed that that's what success in the Forces looked like – dominating as many scoreboards as possible. My conversation with this officer was my first inkling that there was more to leading than simply being first. I realised I could afford to take a little bit of a back step and allow myself to be second or third at some things – to go for ninety per cent rather than one hundred.

At the time, all the lads were preparing for an important test that would assess our knowledge of everything we'd learned to date – fieldcraft, marksmanship principles, camouflage and concealment, the whole lot. I was aware that one skill a lot of the guys had struggled with was a particular way of identifying the cardinal directions. It was known as the 'stick and stone method'. You'd put a stick – a length about a foot and a half would do it – in the ground and mark the tip of the shadow it made with a stone. Then you waited twenty minutes. By that time the shadow would have moved. You'd put another stone where the new tip of the shadow was, and you'd know that the line between your two stones ran east to west.

After my meeting with the officer, I went back to my block, gathered my thoughts for a bit, then approached a gaggle of guys who were chatting in the corner. 'Are any of you lot struggling with the stick and stone method?' I asked them. About five men said yes. Then I went to the next block and asked them. When I'd been round all the blocks, I gave a demonstration outside to at least a dozen lads. This was my first experience of true leadership. And I loved it. The amazing thing was, it began to change me. The more I approached people, the more approachable I became.

I'd only been vaguely aware of it beforehand, but my being on my own all the time had been putting noses out of joint. Back in my army days I'd done the same thing and, as you're about to learn, it had led to disaster. But now, in the Marines, my problem had been picked up through effective training. Not only did that leader give me a new definition of success, he allowed me to enjoy my Marines experience more. Up to that point I'd just been pushing, pushing, pushing, my rev counter constantly in the red. But where can you go from there? And who's with you? You're up there by yourself. If you're alone, who's going to be there for you? Nobody. In the battlefield, that's not a trivial problem.

BUT ALL THESE essential lessons I'd learned with the Marines were still a long way off when I was that still all-too impressionable young lad doing Basic Training at Pirbright. The next chapter of my story wouldn't make itself known until I was in the final fortnight.

I was in my accommodation cleaning my boots when I heard a shout: 'Middleton!' I ran to the door and stood to attention.

'255700 Sapper Middleton reporting for duty.'

'You're wanted in the office, Middleton.'

I marched over to the office and found the commanding officer behind the desk, with his mugs, piles of paperwork and little flags.

I had barely banged out a salute before he said, 'All right, Middleton, come in. We're going to need you on the parade square in a couple of hours, to go through the drill.'

'The drill, sir?'

He looked up at me. 'Yes, Middleton, the drill. For the passing-out parade.'

The passing-out parade? OK. But everyone was going to be at the passing-out parade. Why had he asked only me to go through the drill?

'You'll be picking up your awards,' he said, reading my thoughts. 'So you'll need to familiarise yourself with the ceremony.'

'Awards, sir?'

'Yes, Middleton. Best at physical training. Best all-round recruit. You know, I don't remember anyone ever having won both before. So well done.'

I couldn't help but let off the most enormous grin.

'Have you given any thought to your next move?' he asked me.

'I have, sir,' I said. 'I want to join 9 Parachute Squadron.'

'You want to jump out of planes,' he said.

I smiled again.

'Yes, sir.'

'Very good, Middleton.'

9 Para. Airborne! I couldn't believe it. The opportunity to join this legendary squadron, and wear a maroon beret, was a dream come true. All through training, whenever an

instructor appeared wearing a maroon beret and parachute wings, everyone worshipped him. The Parachute Squadron were above the regular army. It gave you automatic respect. Actually, it was more than respect. It was godlike. Out of all the challenges I could have taken on next, none would be more thrilling than the 'All Arms Parachute Course', which is known as 'P Company'. I'd never been happier, nor had more confidence in my ability to excel. I had absolutely no idea what was waiting for me.

LEADERSHIP LESSONS

Don't let anyone else define who you are. People always make rapid judgements about what sort of person you are from their first impressions, and sometimes these first impressions will be negative. It's so easy to take that on board and simply fall into the mould that other people put you in. Have the strength to realise what's happening and ensure that you define yourself. Meet that negativity with positivity, every single time.

Always have a plan. And make sure that no part of that plan is 'give up'. If I'd had to camp out for a week under a hedge outside Pirbright Camp and wash every day in a stream, then that's what I would have done.

Keep that plan dynamic. Don't be that stubborn leader who, for reasons of pride, refuses to change his plan when new information presents itself. You might think you're asserting your leadership by sticking resolutely to your plan, but you're undermining it. Your team will lose respect for you, and that's the beginning of the end.

Fear of taking action is fear of the unknown. True leaders don't underestimate the potential destructive power of what lies behind that door, but neither do they let that stop them bursting through it, as long as it's done carefully and intelligently.

MAKE YOUR ENEMY
YOUR ENERGY

AND, JUST LIKE that, I was back at the bottom of the pile. When I arrived at 9 Parachute Squadron I was made to feel as if the blue beret and awards I'd been presented with in front of my mother and stepfather at the passing-out parade at Pirbright had all the value of a stone in my shoe.

We'd been instructed to report to Rhine Barracks at Aldershot Garrison, which is popularly known as the 'Home of the British Army' or sometimes 'Aldershot Military Town'. They call it a 'town' because it's enormous. Tipping up there on a blustery morning I could hardly believe the extent of the place. I passed building after building, road after road, and parade squares and offices and flags on poles and rows and rows of blocks of accommodation that held enough beds for more than ten thousand people. The deeper I got into the complex, the more it felt as if I were being swallowed up by some great machine.

But I was also becoming part of that machine. Now that I'd passed Basic Training I was on my way. Before we could get onto P Company, up at the Catterick Garrison in North Yorkshire, I first had to pass what they called 'Pre-Para', a series of physical tests that would prove it was even worth my showing up. I was excited about this new challenge and looking forward to seeing my quarters, finding my little spot and settling in. I wasn't expecting Claridge's – I wasn't even expecting Travelodge – but I knew this would be a bit of an upgrade from what we had to suffer as lowly sprogs down at Pirbright.

After a bit of a hunt, I found the special accommodation block that was kept for trainees. I pushed at the door and glanced inside. I was in the wrong place. I must have been. It was the smell that hit me first. Opening that door unleashed a funky, sour stink of damp and human dirt. Blinking through the foul pea-souper, I saw a concrete floor covered with stained and stinking mattresses and wooden lockers that had been smashed to bits. I knew that paratroopers had the reputation of being tough, grotty and contemptuous of comfort, but you wouldn't let a stray dog sleep in there. I retreated quickly and loitered outside on the kerb until a uniformed man in his forties strode past.

'Excuse me, Sergeant,' I said. 'I'm looking for the trainee accommodation.'

'You've found it,' he said, frowning at the place I'd just exited. 'You a craphat?'

A craphat? I guessed I must have been. 'Yes, Sergeant.'

'Best go make yourself comfortable, then.'

I soon learned that all the Paras called us 'craphats' because, to them, that's all we were. Trainees were seen as too lowly to even speak to. Unless they were doing us some kind of damage, the Paras would not even acknowledge our presence, literally looking through us as if we were invisible. To those guys you were Airborne – or you were shit. And we were definitely shit. And they let us know we were shit by the way they behaved around us, and by thrashing us as hard as they could, in the field and in the gym, every single day of training.

These days the Pre-Para course is led by formally trained, specialist instructors who make sure everything is done correctly, with proper warm-ups and breaks and an eye for the health and safety of the guys. But 1998 was a different era. Back then the whole thing was led in-house by two random lance corporals who'd just happened to have been selected for the task, and probably reluctantly. It seemed as if there were no rules or regulations or standards of care for us craphats that they took seriously – or even knew. This made for a very particular atmosphere that hung over the entire course. It felt dangerous, unstable. Lost in the maze of the Aldershot Military Town, you believed that nobody knew who you were, where you were, or cared what was happening to you, and that the lance corporals could do whatever they wanted to you.

It was those same lance corporals who decided if you were good enough to be sent up to Catterick for the P

Company course. If they thought, for whatever reason, that you weren't ready to make the leap, you'd just have to keep going on Pre-Para … and keep going … and keep going … and keep on fucking going, while praying with every morsel of faith you could find inside you that they'd put you in for the next course. If things went really badly, you'd be 'RTU'd', or 'Returned to Unit'. Getting RTU'd meant they didn't want you in their squadron at all. They'd seen what you had, and had come to the conclusion that there was no point in your persevering with Pre-Para. For me, that would have meant settling for being just an ordinary engineer. There was no way I was going to allow that to happen.

I might have been lighter in build than most of the other lads, and I certainly wasn't as tall, but I was confident I'd make it through – and quickly. My achievements at Pirbright meant nothing here in Aldershot, but that didn't matter. The fact remained that I'd smashed it. It would be a first-time pass for me. I wasn't deluded, and I knew it wasn't going to be easy. It might even be the hardest thing I'd ever done. But the simple truth was I'd never failed at anything physical that had been thrown at me in my life. Couple that with my massive desire to achieve, and there was no way I was going to be hanging around here for long. I'd never wanted anything as badly as this. Every glimpse I'd grabbed of a full-blooded Para, on that first morning at the barracks, had felt like stealing a glimpse of God. To be able to wear the maroon beret and wings that would identify me as a member of the notorious 'Airborne' would feel like the ultimate achievement.

By the time I'd got myself settled in the tramp's nest that was our accommodation, some of the other lads had started drifting in. There were about five new boys who'd turned up that day, all just as hungry as me. The guy sitting on the mattress next to me, it turned out, had been there for a few weeks already.

'Neil Cranston,' he said, introducing himself in a thick Brummy accent. He was a funny-looking lad, with a massive, bouldery head and a tiny face stuck in its middle. His ears looked like a bulldog had been at them, and there was a deep crevasse in the middle of his chin that had a strip of gingery brown hair inside it where his razor couldn't reach.

'Pleased to meet you,' I said. 'Anthony Middleton.' I raised my hand for him to shake, but for some reason Cranston pretended he hadn't seen it. I rubbed it awkwardly on my trousers.

'So tomorrow morning we're going to have to be outside at 6 a.m. sharp, OK?' he said. 'Green T-shirt, DPM (disruptive pattern material, aka camouflage gear) bottoms and your bergen (backpack) filled to forty pounds. There are scales over there in the corner, next to the bin. You'll want to check your weight once you've packed.'

'Great. Thanks, Neil,' I said. 'Cheers for letting me know, mate. So what's it like here?' I flashed him a smile. 'Anything on the room service worth checking out?'

'And don't forget your water bottle,' he said, completely ignoring my friendly attempt at bonding. 'Fill it right up. He'll be checking it too, so give it a good run under the tap, yeah?'

'Sure,' I said. 'Thanks, man. Appreciate it.'

He stood up and walked off. Not the warmest of blokes, I thought, but at least I was now clued in.

The next morning found me out of bed at 5 a.m., present and correct outside at 6 a.m., kit on, bergen packed, water bottle filled all the way up. All the craphats were lined up in formation on a small patch of concrete that was being used as a makeshift parade square. In front of us stood a lance corporal who looked as wide as he was tall.

'To join this squadron you've got to be the best of the best,' he said. 'Every fucker wants to get into 9 Para Squadron, and they want to get in for a reason.'

My gaze drifted to his maroon beret. I felt my body tense in anticipation of the extreme exertion I was about to put it through.

'So if any of you new lads have tipped up here today with the idea that we're about to accept any old shit, you're sorely mistaken. We will begin with a basic fitness test. We'll be doing a mile-and-a-half run and you'd better fucking keep up.'

A run? This was perfect. My legs fizzed with energy. I was a pent-up racehorse. All I wanted to do was launch into the run and show this guy what I had.

'But before we begin, water bottles,' he said. 'Let's see 'em. Come on. Open 'em up.'

We did as he asked, removing the caps and lifting the bottles up gingerly for inspection, making sure we didn't spill a drop. I could hear him going up the line as he checked each one, 'Put it away … put it away … put it away …' Then he got to me. He stopped. He stooped. He peered into my bottle. He grimaced. He smelled of soap and fury. 'What. The. Fuck. Is. That?'

My eyes flickered to my bottle.

'I don't understand, Corporal.'

'Why is your fucking bottle not full to the brim?'

I glanced down at it again, just to make sure I wasn't going mad.

'It is full, Corporal.'

'Get out there,' he said, pointing to a central space on the parade square in front of everyone, 'and pour that fucking water over your head.'

I stepped out, turned to face the lads and did as he asked. The water was absolutely freezing. It ran down my neck and back, trickling down the crack of my arse and hung heavily in the cotton of my T-shirt. All the guys were staring directly ahead of them, showing me the respect of not watching in an obvious way. All except Cranston, that is, who was eyeballing me throughout with a subtle but undeniably smug expression on his face.

'Now go and fill it up to the brim,' said the lance corporal.

I bolted back up the stairs to the accommodation, the saturated material of my T-shirt slapping against my skin, and ran the bottle under the tap again. I made sure not to panic, to take my time, and to make sure it was absolutely as full as it could be. No more than forty seconds later I was back out in front of the lance corporal on the parade square again.

'Middleton!' he shouted. 'Are you fucking stupid or are you fucking deaf? I said full to the brim.'

It was full. It was touching the brim. It really was. There was literally no way I could get it any fuller.

'I don't understand, Corporal.'

'Get out there and pour it over your fucking head.'

I poured the water over my head again, trying to avoid Cranston's shithawk squint. What the hell was going on? Why was I being singled out? How had I highlighted myself? I took a guess that the lance corporal checked my records. Maybe he'd seen how well I'd done at Pirbright and was putting me in my place. Or what if it was worse than that? What if he was trying to break me?

'Now fill it up to the brim,' he said.

I ran up the stairs again. Painstakingly, I made sure every last drop of water entered the bottle and, with the care of a master watchmaker, gently fastened the lid.

Forty seconds later: 'Are you deaf or fucking stupid? Pour it over your fucking head.'

When I'd tipped four full bottles of freezing water over

me and somehow managed not to show one glimmer of distress, he finally relented.

'Will one of you craphats show this dickhead how it's done?'

That evening one of the lads demonstrated the proper technique. You had to fill a bath with water, fully submerge the bottle, bang it to get all the bubbles out, then put the lid on in the bath, with the bottle still underwater. That was the only way you could get it filled up to his standards. And that wasn't all. When the lance corporal came round to inspect it, you had to squeeze the bottle a little bit so the level came right up to the brim. Everybody knew how it was done except me.

I couldn't believe that Cranston hadn't told me this the night before, and then had rolled around in every second of my humiliation like a pig in shit. But, I told myself, at least the lance corporal hadn't been singling me out. On the contrary, he was teaching me something that I've never since forgotten. It's the attention to detail that's important, even with something that seems so irrelevant as having your water touching the bottle's brim. On the battlefield, those last two sips might be the ones that save your life. I've carried that lesson through my career. If you fuck up the small things, it leads to a big fucking disaster.

But this wasn't much help to me during our Basic Fitness Test that morning. By the time I finally started out on the first mile-and-a-half run I had four bottles of freezing water hanging in my hair and clothes, and was wet, cold and humiliated. I realised right then that I could either allow what had happened to eat away at me or I could use it. Rather than trying to squash the anger, I let it grow. It became an energy. With every stride I visualised Cranston's smug look, turning his animosity and betrayal into a battery that powered me. This, I knew instinctively, was the best revenge I could have possibly taken.

Despite the events of that morning I managed to come in second. Cranston, meanwhile, had finished somewhere near the back. At the end of a hard morning's PT, we filed in for lunch. As ever, I sat alone on the corner of a table with a beaker of water and my rice and fish. Over my shoulder I could hear some of the boys talking to Cranston about me. 'That Ant's a fit lad,' someone said. I couldn't make out what he came back with, but I ate the rest of my meal happily. It wouldn't be long until I'd be far away from that loser, earning my maroon beret up at Catterick. No doubt he'd be RTU'd before long and I'd never see him again.

After lunch it was time for another run, but this time with weighted bergens on our backs. They call it 'tabbing' – Tactical Advance to Battle. We had eight miles to cover with the forty-pound bergens we'd packed the night before using appropriate kit, a combination of our sleeping bag, mess tins, rations – anything we'd actually take into the field as a serving Para. At the allotted time we reported to the lance corporal, all lined up in formation once again with our bergens between our feet. On one side of him was a duty recruit with a set of scales. Spine straight and chin up, I watched the lance corporal going round, lifting up the bergens one by one and weighing them. He and his partner had arranged themselves so only they could see the result on the scales. This was no accident. It meant each one of us was shitting ourselves until the moment we were nodded through.

It was all I could do not to break out into a huge smile when Cranston's bergen came in a pound under. 'Go and get a rock,' the lance corporal told him. He pointed to a particularly large specimen beneath a tree in a small patch of greenery on the other side of the road. As Cranston waddled back with it, I realised it must have added at least ten pounds to his bergen. Soon it was my turn. As I watched them lift my bergen onto the scales, I noticed Cranston was showing as much interest in the result as I was. A thought flitted through my head – maybe he's tampered with it. For the longest two seconds, the lance corporal didn't say anything. 'All right, put it on your back,' he said, finally. Thank God for that.

Then, the second our bergens had all been weighed, it began. 'Follow me!' shouted the lance corporal. With that, he and the duty recruit set off. And when I say 'set off' I mean, boom, they were gone, as if on rockets, out of the parade square, out of the base and into a massive military training area that must have covered at least twenty square miles. And I kept up with them. I made sure I did. For the first two miles. But then, at first almost unnoticeably but soon undeniably, I started flagging. 'I can run,' I thought to myself as my knees pumped and sweat ran down my neck, 'I know I can run. But this weight is killing me.'

It took me a while to realise why it was so much easier for the others. The problem was my height. My legs were relatively short, which meant that I had to work that much harder. Whereas they could quickly stride, I had to sprint. Not that there was any point in making excuses. Tabbing was part of Pre-Para for a good reason: you go into operations with the weight that you need to survive on your back. You carry what it takes to sustain yourself in a war zone. If you couldn't keep pace it meant you didn't have what it took. It was as simple as that. There was no free pass for height, just as there was no free pass for the physically weak or the unmotivated. And I had no argument with that at all.

But still, I was finding it exhausting. With every step I took, the weight of the bergen shot up my calves into my chest, and seemed to punch another lump of energy out of me. And I knew there was a whole lot worse to come. The muddy track eventually took me to the base of a climb that I'd already heard all about. This one was legendary. Craphat Hill was called Craphat Hill because it eats Craphats. The sight of it bearing down on me swiped at my faltering energy like a bear's paw. On my left I heard the breath of another lad about to overtake me. I turned. It was Cranston, who was still going hard with that big rock in his bergen. 'You can run with fuck-all weight on your back,' he panted, 'but you're shit now, aren't you?' What strength I had left melted away. I looked up. I couldn't believe what I was seeing. Craphat Hill was pretty much vertical. Desperately, I glanced behind me. With a sinking sense of shame and horror I realised I was last.

And that was how it went, first for days and then for weeks. Whenever we had tabbing I came in last, panting, short and sorry, every single time. Ironically, being last was a first for me. I hadn't felt anything like this since I'd been bullied back at school. I began to dread tabbing. Perhaps because I'd highlighted myself by doing so well in that first race, some of the guys seemed to take a special pleasure in seeing me brought down to size. Usually led by Cranston, they began giving me a hard time back at the accommodation. It started as stage whispers in my presence – 'What the fuck is he still doing here?' Before long, people were up and in my face. 'Just fuck off back to your unit, Ant,' they'd say. 'Give it up. You're not going to make it.'

I knew they wanted a fight, and I knew Cranston was in the middle of it. But there was nothing I could do but try to maintain my strength of character. Just as it had been with Ivan in Pirbright, I wasn't going to let them push me into being someone else. Despite how they were acting, I treated them with the very respect they were finding it so hard to extend to me.

At least things were going better outside of the tabbing. I was running well with nothing on my back and smashing it in the gym. I was pretty certain my success in these areas was the only reason I hadn't been RTU'd yet. But the instructors would only let me get away with that for so long. The clock was ticking for me – and I knew it. The undeniable fact was that I was showing no signs of improvement.

Every four weeks we'd be made to line up outside the corporal's office. One by one we'd be called in. On the corporal's desk there'd be two items. On the left there was the coveted maroon beret that paras call their 'machine'. On the right there was a glass of sour milk. If the decision had been made to send you up to Catterick, you were told to touch the beret. If you'd not made it, you'd sniff the milk. I was getting sick of it. Every time, I was being told, 'Middleton, smell the milk.' And then, one week, I was waiting my turn when I saw Cranston exiting with his face lit up like fireworks night. He didn't even have to say anything. It was obvious. Cranston had touched the maroon machine.

Meanwhile, up on Craphat Hill, practice wasn't making perfect. The tabbing was getting harder, not easier. My feet were becoming badly damaged and, because everyone else was striding while I was running, my bergen was sliding from side to side against my lower and upper back. Everybody suffers from what they call 'bergen burns', but mine were on a different level. Across large swathes of my back my skin had pretty much worn away, so I'd spend my evenings carefully strapping my wounds with black tape.

When I was running I simply tried to shut out the pain. What else could I do?

But there was one truly bright spot in my Pre-Para schedule. Most weekends I'd actually be able to get out of Aldershot. I'd leave the barracks and travel down to Portsmouth to stay with my nan, partly to get away from the squalor and the terrible food, partly to get away from Cranston and his pals. I didn't want to burden nan with my problems, or spoil our time together by being negative, but I knew she was wondering why I was still around and not in Catterick because she'd ask these little probing questions that I'd have to bat away.

But then, one Saturday night, after months of punishment on Pre-Para, I sat down at the dinner table for my favourite meal of sausage, cabbage and mash and, forgetting myself, I accidentally winced in pain.

'What's the matter, Anthony?'

'Nothing, Nan,' I smiled. 'Let's tuck in. This looks amazing.'

'What's wrong, love? Are you in pain? Is it your back?'

'It's nothing,' I said. 'Are these sausages from the butcher? They're a decent size.'

'Show me,' she said. 'You never know, I might be able to help.'

I tried to distract her with a bit more of my sausages talk, then I tried laughing it off, but I knew she wasn't going to take no for an answer. Reluctantly, I stood up, turned around and peeled my shirt up to show her. There were scabs, scars and bloody, weeping wounds under there. Whole layers of skin were missing.

'Oh, darling,' she said, trying to control her voice. 'What are they doing to you?'

I pulled my shirt back down again and shrugged. 'It's what I want, Nan,' I said.

'But why, Anthony?'

'I want to join 9 Para Squadron and this is what you have to do. It's normal. It's nothing that's going to kill me.'

'You don't have to prove anything to anyone,' she said. 'You don't have to be a paratrooper.'

'But I can't just be a normal engineer, Nan,' I said.

'Why? Why can't you?'

'Because I have to get my wings,' I said with a shrug. I picked up my knife and fork again and began to attack my dinner. When I looked up, Nan's eyes had turned bloodshot and wet.

That night, as I lay in bed, I thought about what she'd said. How could I explain why I wanted to earn my wings so badly? It was like trying to explain why green is green or why Cranston was a dick. It was obvious, wasn't it? The Paras were the best. They were gods. Who doesn't want to be a god? And it was more than that, too. It felt like my destiny, to wear those wings on my shoulder and the maroon machine and the Pegasus insignia that showed I belonged to 5 Airborne Brigade, of which 9 Parachute

Squadron was a part, and to walk among those gods as an equal.

I hadn't ever really questioned why I wanted it, nor whether or not it could happen. But I'd been on Pre-Para for months now and, if anything, it was getting harder. Perhaps, I thought, it just wasn't going to happen. The lads back at base seemed to all be in agreement. And, you know, what would happen if I did decide to quit? It would be my business, and my business only. The reason I was coming last was simple – my legs weren't long enough, and I couldn't help that. Perhaps I'd be wiser just to accept it. I should listen to my nan. She's been around for a while and knew a bit about the world. 'Go to a normal engineer regiment,' I told myself. 'Stick to your strengths.'

The next morning I awoke feeling flat and tired, but relieved to have finally come to a decision. I gave Nan a hug goodbye and pulled my bag over my shoulder, now flinching openly at the pain.

'I've been thinking,' I said. 'You're right. I'm not built for it. It's my legs. Nothing's gonna change that, no matter how much I want to wish it away.'

I was expecting her to look pleased, but she just sighed. It was confusing. Had I disappointed her?

Back at the barracks the next morning it was more of the same. Out once again with the heavy bergen, eight miles of raw pain, all the way up Craphat Hill, dragging myself across the hellish Seven Sisters, pushing myself through what they called the 'Hole in the Wall', which involved crawling through a pit of stinking mud that was full of smashed glass bottles that civilians would throw into it, then squeezing through a narrow gap in a brick wall. As I slogged, I stewed over my nan's reaction. I knew she had my best interests at heart, but I also felt that she thought I was better than that. What should I do? I couldn't just chant a magic spell and put ten fucking inches on my legs.

I came last again, that day. It was my worst time ever. As I was catching my breath, alone by the wagon, one of the lance corporals beckoned me over. 'Middleton, come here,' he said. I staggered over to where he was standing. 'Listen, lad, you've got the drive and will, nobody can take that away from you. It's why you're still here. But you're too small. You're not like the others. You haven't got the build.' There was nothing I could say to that but, 'OK, Corporal.'

As the wagon bounced us back towards the barracks, I watched the mud track and military fencing pass by outside the canopy. I finally decided that that was it. They were obviously going to RTU me soon, and I might as well go out with dignity and save them the trouble. I imagined Cranston's expression when he found out, that nasty grin. 'You're not like the others,' the lance corporal had said. Not like Cranston? Not as good as him? I found myself filling with a sense of angry defiance. And then something odd happened. The angrier I felt, the more the pain in my back seemed to fade away. I remembered how I'd got through that first Basic

Fitness Test by using my hatred of him as a source of energy. I focused on him, hard. I felt pumped. Violent. By the time the wagon pulled up, I was almost ready to ask the driver to turn around and take me back to Craphat Hill, so I could do the tab again.

Just by chance, another new intake arrived two days later. One of the boys happened to be slightly overweight, and this meant that the limelight, finally, was taken off me. It also meant that I didn't come in last. As well as using my rage at Cranston to fire me up, I allowed myself to use someone else's struggle as my strength. With each tab, from thereon in, I slowly became better and better. That improvement was one hundred per cent psychological. I started climbing the ladder again, getting faster and faster, closer and closer to the front. And before I knew it, there were probably two or three of us going on the next course, and it seemed clear I was going to be one of them.

That experience gave me a lesson I've never forgotten, and it's one I still use regularly. Your enemy is fuel. He is energy. Hatred can be the most powerful motivator there is. In life you'll always come across jealous and negative people, or people who simply don't believe in you. Every single one of them is a Duracell battery. Plug them in. Give yourself that edge by using their own electricity against them. Success isn't only the most satisfying form of revenge – it's the only positive one there is.

*   *   *

BUT USING YOUR enemies like this can also be dangerous. I only truly learned this during my time in the Royal Marines, many years after my endless struggles up Craphat Hill. It was just before lunch on a sunny day in July, and I'd returned from a session on Woodbury Common military training area. I was outside my accommodation block removing the twigs, leaves and grass from my gillie suit, and was about to go back inside when a young guy I'd been chatting to a few days previously in the mess hall passed by.

'Hey, Ant, did you hear about that Marine who died in Afghan?' he said.

My heart thumped. 'Who is it?' I asked.

He shrugged his shoulders. 'Don't know. It's going around the drill quarters. They're planning the funeral back in the office. Right in the middle of it now. Didn't get a name. I was wondering if you knew?'

'No, mate. No idea.'

Once he'd left I paced as quickly as I could to the Sniper Troop office and knocked on his door.

'I'm sorry to disturb you,' I said. 'But I've just heard that one of the lads has caught it up in Afghanistan. Is it true?'

'I can confirm that,' he said.

'Who is it?'

'I can't say any names, Middleton,' he said. 'We haven't released the news to his family yet.'

'Mate, please.'

There was a long silence.

'What I can say,' he eventually replied, 'is that he liked to juggle.'

This was impossible. It was Lewis. He was a good friend. I'd got to know and trust him during my counter-terrorist sniper course, but everyone at Lympstone knew of him. He was unusually well-spoken, relentlessly positive and a bit kooky. It wouldn't be unusual to see him walking through the accommodation blocks in rest periods practising his favourite hobby, which was juggling. Sometimes he'd be throwing sparkly balls around the air, sometimes knives. If you met Lewis in the street, you might guess that he was a lawyer or a kindly geography teacher. In fact, he was one of the most efficiently deadly men in the British services.

Of course, deaths like his were part of the deal. You heard about military people being killed in action all the time. But it was a shock to hear that one of our guys had caught it up. There was just something about being an operator that made you feel invincible. It sometimes felt as if we could dodge bullets. All I could do for the next few minutes was sit on the edge of my bed, looking at my phone. I wondered how it had happened. Enemy fire? An IED? A corrupt Afghan who'd been employed by the British military? There were plenty of stories of those flying about. Ten minutes later I stood up, brushed myself off and began preparing for the afternoon's exercise. Because what else could I do?

Within the week, Lewis's body had been repatriated. Ten days after I heard the news, I arrived at a huge, dark, stone cathedral for his funeral. He was sent off with full military honours, including a ten-gun salute and a ceremonial flyover by two Hawk jets after the service. I was invited to join the burial party too, about an hour and a half's drive from the cathedral, and be one of the pall bearers. There were only ten of us there, including the family. I watched his wife and two daughters, aged eight and ten, stand beside the dark, damp, black hole in the ground. I couldn't get the thought out of my head – their husband and dad was going in there. They read poems and managed to somehow hold themselves together. I was struck not only by their courage but by the endless depth of their love for their man who was now gone.

When the time came to finally say goodbye, the coffin was lifted into the air by ropes. I removed the metal stands from beneath it and guided it over the pit. Then, slowly, it was lowered in. Lewis's family stepped forward to throw roses into the ground. They tossed in handfuls of dirt that clattered on top of the coffin. That was when it became too much. The daughters broke, sobbing desperately, their hands pressed to their faces, tears leaking out from between pale fingers. It was hard to know how they'd ever learn to live without him. Maybe they wouldn't. Their despair was such that it felt like a fog that had escaped from their hearts and was enveloping all of us.

Y YOUR ENERGY

the bravery of Lewis's wife,
for the sake of her children.
I approached her.

an,' I said. 'If there's anything
, we're always here.'

. I could tell she wasn't really
t she was going through was
me protective instinct in her
he moment. Glassy eyed, she
nk you, thank you.'

when something stopped me.
wis's death is not going to go

focus and looked back at me
said simply, 'Good.'

istan, the loss of our friend
lt ever-present, pushing us
tor. All I wanted was to get
ge for his wife and girls. The
ost overwhelmed me. I could
of just wanting to kill every-
here on patrol were to blame.
hint of a threat or the slight-
o aim and fire at. For a while
range thing was, I'd also meet
nd be eating bread with them
ldn't be thinking like that at

all. But then, as soon as I'd left their compounds, I'd be back in the zone, thinking, 'All right, you fuckers.' I wanted to mow them all down.

Most people don't understand hatred. The truth is we need it. Hatred is why we're motivated to defend ourselves. Hatred of fascism and hatred of communism got us through the twentieth century with our values intact, just as hatred of radical Islamism and the terrorism it breeds are getting us through our problems today. Hatred is a natural human instinct. We have it for a reason. But it's a dangerous tool that needs using with wisdom, strength and delicacy. You need the presence of mind to tap into it just enough that it serves you, but not so much that it twists you up and throws you into a dark place.

But that's what started happening in Afghanistan. Lewis's death had made it personal for everyone who knew him. The hatred it generated caused many of them to make bad decisions. When I got out there all I heard was, 'If they've got a weapon on them, they're a bad guy. Just take them out, even if they pose a minimal threat. Just do what you've got to do.' I felt exactly like they did, but I didn't want to be a bully with a weapon. When that mindset runs away with you, you're in war crimes territory. I'm not judging any of them. I know how it feels. I'm not exaggerating when I say that, at times, I felt like a dog with bloodlust. Getting my head back under control was one of the toughest challenges of my military career.

It's the kind of energy that can eat you from the inside. If you internalise your enemies too much, they can begin to obsess you to the extent that you become both defensive and aggressive, the kind of person nobody wants to be around. I met a character who personified this perfectly when I was filming Series 2 of *SAS: Who Dares Wins* at an old military base in the Ecuadorian jungle. Geoff was a satellite installer and former drug addict who'd been deported from Australia after some sort of violent incident. He'd also served six months in prison.

From the moment I first laid eyes on him, on morning number one, I knew everything about him that I needed to. All the contestants were lined up in formation in our makeshift parade square, which was surrounded with military buildings and corrugated roofs. I'd decided to welcome them into the challenge with the opposite of a motivational speech.

'This environment is brutal,' I said. 'It's hostile. It's claustrophobic. It will chew you up and spit you out. This environment is enough to break most of you. If you fight it will fuck you up. Trust me. If I have to babysit any of you, we'll just fuck you off. We want individuals who can look after themselves. You're ours for the next nine days. Embrace it, gentlemen.'

As I was talking, I was checking out all their body language. Geoff's attitude problem simply exploded out of him. Just the way he was standing told me he had a major problem with authority. He was a short guy and he was broad. When I began asking questions, the other lads would reply snappily with, 'Yes, Staff!' But when I questioned Geoff, all I got was, 'Yep. Yep.' Here, I realised, was the classic problem child. He was completely possessed by all those perceived enemies that he carried around inside him. They were controlling his every thought and action. He wasn't using them as an energy – they were using him.

I decided to get straight in there and push his buttons. The 'mirror room' is what we called the converted shipping container where we carried out our interrogations. Contestants would be called in without warning. A black bag and goggles would be put over their heads and they'd be manhandled through a complex series of turns to completely disorientate them. The next thing they'd know, they'd be sitting in front of a table, on the other side of which would be me and another member of the directing staff.

On that very first evening I sent the order for him to see us. I was joined by a gifted former SAS operative, Mark 'Billy' Billingham.

'There's something quite unsettling about you,' I told Geoff. 'I can't quite put my finger on it. You seem like quite an unpredictable character. I know a loose cannon when I see one. There's a switch in you. And when it goes you can't control it.'

Billy began probing into his past. It soon emerged that Geoff had been a drug dealer.

'Did you have fucking conscience?' he asked him.

'No,' replied Geoff defiantly. 'I didn't give a shit.'

Now we were getting somewhere. Here was the real Geoff. It hadn't taken long. Billy increased the pressure.

'Did you ever calculate in your fucking stupid mind how many families' lives you fucked up?'

Geoff took a sharp breath, dipped his head and ran his hand slowly over the top of it. This was it. He was breaking.

'Er, yeah, no,' he mumbled.

'You've got a daughter,' I said. 'How old's your daughter?'

'Fourteen.'

'Does she do drugs?'

Billy was going for the jugular. Geoff tried not to rise.

'Does she do drugs?' Billy said. 'I asked you a question.'

'I know you asked me a question but it's a stupid fucking question.'

This guy was a hand grenade and he was seconds away from going off. The situation would need careful control. I knew from his size and his past – and from the masculine power that was tasing off him – that if he kicked off he was going to be a handful. I had to assert a bit of dominance. I rose from my seat and stood over him, quickly sending him a message: It's probably best not to start anything because, if that happens, it's not going to end nicely for you.

'Relax,' I told him. 'Relax yourself. Why do you think we're pushing your buttons? Calm it down. If you were caught in a hostile environment and you reacted the way you've just reacted, do you know what would happen to you? You'd get a bullet in the back of your head.'

What he didn't realise was that none of this was necessarily an issue for me. It didn't matter to me that he was a problem child. I didn't even mind the attitude. I can work on these problems and even take great pleasure in rectifying them. What I didn't know was whether he could help himself.

The fact is that the Special Forces are looking for men who are on that razor edge. A lot of us were – and are – just like Geoff. For many men of the SAS and SBS, if they'd taken one step to the left at a certain point in life they'd have ended up in prison. A lot of us were constantly teetering on the point of self-destruction. We could either control that self-destructive urge or just press the button – and often our finger was hovering just a millimetre above it. That was definitely true of me. The people in charge know full well that this dynamic exists within us. It's the reason they want us, the reason we get results. It's how we've passed Special Forces Selection. But they take you with their fingers crossed behind their backs, just hoping and praying that the button doesn't get pressed.

We left Geoff to stew overnight on what had happened. The next morning he was late to the parade ground. The contestants were given a strict timing for breakfast, between 6 and 6.30, and they all had to go together. As they were eating, I inspected their accommodation. Someone had left their toothbrush and toothpaste on their bed, while everyone else had packed all their kit properly away. As soon as I saw it, I knew it had to be Geoff. He'd left me a gift. And I capitalised on it straight away.

When they filed back from breakfast, I stood outside their accommodation, blocking their way. Once they'd all gathered, I told them, 'I want you to walk around in there and I don't want you to touch anything. I just want you to inspect the accommodation and point at the bed that's not right.' They all saw it.

'Whose is it?'

'Geoff's.'

I knew he'd been raging all night and that this was going to tip him over the cliff.

'You've just fucked up there, haven't you?' I told him. 'What makes you so special? You think you're special, do you? Right, everyone out on the parade ground.'

I got hold of a foam roll mat, of the type you use for camping, and instructed everyone to stand round it.

'I want you all in the press-up position,' I said. I pointed Geoff to the mat. 'Come and lie down,' I said. 'Relax. Chill.' But that he couldn't deal with it.

'Fuck you. You're pissing me off now, fucking prick,' he said, tearing his armband off and thus instantly ordering his plane ticket back to the UK.

The thing is, I'd only have made him lie on that mat for five minutes. And if he'd been man enough, I'd have decided that he was getting it and that I could work on him. I genuinely wanted to bring him back into the fold, but now I couldn't. I decided to have a chat with him in the medical room as he was being checked over before his flight home. I could see he was still raging. I braced myself for a physical fight, sitting down lightly on the edge of a medical bed, my arms and legs tensed, primed and ready to spring into action.

'You've got so much potential, but you're a fucking hand grenade,' I said. 'You're unpredictable, and that makes you unreliable. What frustrates me is that you've turned your life around. But you can turn it right back upside down again with the flick of a switch. You love your daughter. But you won't be any good to her when you're in the fucking nick.'

'What it all boils down to is weakness,' he admitted. 'You know as well as I do. I thought if I can get through this I might actually be able to trust myself. But I don't.'

He broke down in tears. I'd been Geoff's enemy that morning. It was my gift to him. He should have used me. He should have shown me. But rather than draw energy from me, he'd allowed me to eat him up.

There's one other situation in which I've learned that it's useful to build yourself through confrontation, and that's in conditions of extreme pain. You have to learn to cope with pain on the battlefield, where you may well find yourself having to walk on a broken ankle or with a leg that's got a bullet in it – or be killed. I've learned that it's useful to make your own body the enemy, to focus on what's causing you grief and fire fury back at it. I'll have a voice going around my head: 'You fucking think you hurt, do you? I'll fucking show you.'

Not long ago I was invited to a team-building event with 30 Commando, down at Stonehouse Barracks in Plymouth. As part of the day I'd agreed to take part in a morning of Brazilian jiu-jitsu. But the week before I'd broken the big toe on my right foot. There was no way I was going to pull out of my commitment, but twenty minutes after I started grappling on the mat I felt my toe break again. It was agony. And I knew I was going to be rolling around for another two hours. So I separated myself from it. I turned my toe into my enemy and went into battle with it. 'You want fucking pain do you? You don't know what fucking pain is. Try this.' At the end of every round I'd surreptitiously smash it into the ground or walk up to the wall and, when no one was looking, kick it. 'I've got a job to do and you fucking think you can stop me doing my job, do you? Right, have some of this.' Pain is an aggressive feeling and, to be on top of it, you have to get aggressive with it right back.

Most people have never been to their limits, so they don't know what lies there. I've been to my limits and beyond, so I know my body. I know what it can do. I know I can get to a point where my mind and body are screaming, 'Fucking stop!' and I'll reply, 'Fucking stop, you cunt? Watch this.' Pain isn't telling you what to do. Pain is asking you a question. All you have to do is say no.

THE MOST SURPRISING thing about the three-week P Company course in Catterick was that, after the misery of Pre-Para, it was a breeze. It was three weeks of races, assault courses and trainasium height training, which involved things like walking across the tops of thirty-foot poles. I loved it. But I wasn't quite a paratrooper yet. Because I'd not yet done my 'jumps course', I was what they called a 'penguin' – a bird that can't fly. But the jumps course wouldn't be a challenge in the way that Pre-Para was. It wasn't something that people ever really failed. On the contrary, I couldn't wait to get on it.

So I returned to Aldershot from Catterick feeling as if I'd truly earned my maroon beret. Perhaps because my struggle had been so great – it was the first time I'd really been tested – I'd never had more confidence. But I was spending my days with some of the same people who'd watched me struggling so badly. People like Cranston. He'd classed me as a loser when I'd been there before. I hoped that now I'd returned, and I'd proved him and everyone else wrong, it would be a new start. I, for one, wouldn't hold the past against him.

On that first day back we went on an eight-mile troop run. I was comfortably at the front when two of the lads sped up behind me, a lance corporal and Cranston. 'What are you doing at the front?' said the lance corporal. I pushed on, trying to put some distance back between us, but Cranston threw his foot out, kicking my leg right behind the knee. I tumbled forward, falling into a ditch, the left side of my face taking the brunt.

'You think you're the fucking man, but you've just come back from P Company,' he shouted over his shoulder as he sped down the track. 'Fucking sprog.'

I pushed myself back on my feet and spent the rest of the run in the centre of the pack. I was fuming. Be at the back, and they single you out. Be at the front, and they single you out. I'd joined the army to excel. I'd imagined I was going to be surrounded by like-minded people. But it was beginning to seem as if the only place you could really get on was right here in the middle.

And so that's what I did. I sat back. What was the point in pushing myself when I wasn't even going to be allowed to get there? All that mattered to them was that I was a sprog. That was the be-all and end-all. There was an iron hierarchy in place that had nothing to do with skill and everything do to with gang-law and favouritism. The people at the top were the ones who'd been there for longer or who had the right friends. They were 'the boys'. They'd go down the pub and drink and fight, and that's how it was all decided. It was all stitched up.

So what else could I do? I knew their game. And I had no choice but to play it.

LEADERSHIP LESSONS

Make your enemy your energy. The fact of the matter is, becoming a leader often means creating enemies. It's a fight to get to that top spot, and not everyone is going to be happy that you've beaten them. They're going to turn their resentment into negativity that they'll fire at you in an attempt to bring you down. You have a choice. Allow that negativity in, and let it obsess you and eventually poison you. Or turn it around. If you're smart, these enemies become a gift – a battery that never runs out.

A lesson is a lesson. No matter how it comes to you, even if it's in an apparently negative package, take that lesson as a positive. Of course I didn't enjoy having to pour freezing water over my head over and over again that morning. And I was unhappy when I realised none of the lads had told me the correct procedure for filling the bottle. But I've never forgotten the lesson I was taught: attention to detail. If you get the small things wrong, big problems will find you.

These lessons never stop. If you're paying attention, you'll have a learning moment every day. Make a habit of spending two minutes before turning your lights out, every night, working out what the lesson of the day has been. Go to sleep with the satisfaction that, having now learned it, you'll wake up as a better version of yourself than you've been the previous day.

There's always a route around your weakness. We all have things about us that we can't change. A part of the reason I struggled at Pre-Para was the length of my legs. Rather than throw my hands up, which I very nearly did, I realised I could compensate in another area. We all have reasons to make excuses for failure. Most people use them. Be the exceptional person – find the route around.

LEADERS STAND APART FROM CROWDS

MY NEXT TASK was to kill the penguin. That would happen over the course of four weeks at RAF Brize Norton in Oxfordshire, where I'd learn to jump out of aeroplanes and, by doing so, earn my wings. Even before I arrived I'd vowed to put Cranston and the others behind me. Any negativity that might have been lingering in my head vanished completely as I was driven through those gates on a Monday morning, proudly wearing my maroon beret.

It was a thrill just to be there. RAF Brize Norton is a huge air base in Oxfordshire that has over six thousand people living and working on it. It's also a place that's redolent with history. And it was from here that essential parachute and glider operations commenced later in the Second World War. On D-Day, brave fighters took off from Brize Norton to land in northern France to successfully capture bridges and German battery installations. Many of the men who set off from this base to kill Nazis and to free Europe were members of the Parachute Regiment. And now I was a member of the Airborne family too. Pretty much.

One of the many little visual cues that marks the elite regiments like the Paras or the Commandos from the others is that we'd wear a peak in our berets. On my second day I found myself happily strolling from the accommodation over to the NAAFI, where there were a few shops and a bar, when I saw a young guy approaching with a decidedly cocky walk. He was wearing a blue beret – with a peak in it. The feeling hit me sooner than the thought: who the fuck did this kid think he was? This was a serious breach of protocol. How was he getting away with it? Why had nobody bollocked him? In reality, the only real difference between me and this young man was that I'd done a three-week course. But those three weeks mattered. 'Who the fuck do you think you are?' I thought, as I approached him. 'Fucking craphat.'

It wasn't in my nature to say anything, but as I got nearer to the delusional craphat I found myself aggressively staring at him. As he got closer I realised he looked familiar. It was hard to see, with the sun in my eyes, so I had to slow down to a near stop. I couldn't believe it. Was it really possible? It couldn't be. The craphat with the peak was my elder brother Michael.

'Fucking hell, Mike!' I cried, immediately forgetting about his beret. 'What are you doing here?'

'What am I doing here?' he said. 'I'm in the fucking RAF, you knobhead. What are you doing here?'

Of course, I knew my elder brother had just joined the Forces. It just hadn't occurred to me that he'd be here, at Brize Norton.

It was amazing to have someone who felt like an ally by my side at last. But it felt even better to have someone I cared about see me in my maroon beret and the Pegasus insignia that showed I belonged to the Paras. The last time I'd seen Mike I'd been a nobody. Now I was a member of 9 Para – the Engineers. Whereas it was the duty of 1, 2 and 3 Para to fight, ours was to build bridges and clear mines and demolish infrastructure. This is why we were known for being physically strong and for breaking stuff. With that, we developed a reputation for being the rogues of the army. We brought an impressive level of destruction and madness everywhere we went. So what else could I do? If destruction and madness was the rule of my new tribe, then destruction and madness was what I would have to bring. I was determined to uphold the traditions of my badge. I wasn't going to let the legend of 9 Para down, especially in the eyes of my elder brother.

And so began the most brilliant and raucous four weeks I'd ever had. From that moment on, Mike and I were inseparable, and we went around the base being total menaces. We'd steal bicycles and pedal them around camp, we'd smash windows, we'd ride off on people's motorbikes and chuck them over walls. I started having fun with the women, having several on the go at once. I'd creep out of one door in the women's accommodation and nip four doors down to see someone else. One night, I was running out of one bedroom when I saw Mike emerging from the room next to me. But despite the pandemonium I found myself at the centre of, when it came to dealing with people one on one I remained my old polite and respectful self. It was partly because of this that we never really got into proper trouble. But it was also because our particular brand of misbehaviour, over that period, was relatively harmless.

After receiving my wings at Brize Norton I was sent on my first deployment. I'd be going to Northern Ireland. It was exciting to finally be leaving the country and heading into the world as a member of 9 Parachute Squadron. As we boarded the Boeing C-17 plane for take-off, it all suddenly felt real. My excitement didn't last long. Although we went on street patrols now and then, this was 1999 and things were a lot quieter than they had been ten or twenty years previously. There simply wasn't much happening out there. Most of my time was taken up assisting in the demolition of the notorious Maze Prison in County Antrim. Because I'd only had my wings for a couple of months, I was still seen as a sprog. This meant I wasn't given any of the more responsible or interesting jobs. I wasn't up in any of the big machines, knocking down walls. Instead I was down in the ditches, lugging rubble and hardcore, caked in sweat and dust, and covered in blisters and cuts. It was genuine, old-fashioned man work. At the end of every shift I felt like I was emerging from a long day deep in a coal mine, filthy, knackered and sore.

Back at the barracks, we lads from the Airborne were making our presence felt. We quickly colonised the NAAFI bar. Anyone who wasn't Airborne was made to feel distinctly unwelcome. We were loud, rowdy and intimidating. The shared belief was that if you weren't a Para, you weren't worthy to be in the bar when we were there. There were twenty or so of us who'd take up the physical space with our volume and behaviour, and if any stubborn remainers insisted on defying us and drinking in the corner, someone would front up to them: 'Listen, fuck off, this is a fucking Airborne bar now.'

I was nineteen years old and built like a whippet. Two pints of Heineken would leave me fairly wrecked. But I had no option but to keep chugging away and try desperately to keep up with the older lads, not least the squadron's big alpha male, who everyone called Bus, because he was built like the smelly end of a London double-decker. Bus was your typical bully. A big lad. He liked to throw his weight around, he wasn't scared of anything and he always wanted everyone to know that he was the most Airborne of the Airborne. One night, I was four pints in and blearily watching a game of pool when I became aware of Bus talking to a group of lads over by the cigarette machine. Bus smirked and then they all smirked and, one by one, looked around at me. Something was going on.

I pretended to be completely focused on the pool game as three of them barged their way behind the bar and pulled the top tray out of a steaming glass-washer. A group of nine or ten men gathered around the dance floor, too many of them throwing hungry looks in my direction for me to feel in any way comfortable. They began hurling their beer, glasses and all, onto the wooden floor. Glass smashed everywhere and alcohol spattered up the walls. Then Bus started handing out more glasses from the wire tray. They started throwing them down too.

Bus walked up to me. 'Initiation time, sprog,' he leered. A low cheer arose from the group. Bus grabbed my upper arm and pulled me to the top of the dance floor, now slicked with alcohol and broken glass. Circling dots of light from the disco ball picked their way over thousands of glinting splinters and terrifying upright shards that curved into the air like great shark's teeth.

'Head first,' shouted Bus. 'Dive in, boy.' The cheer rose louder. Bus turned to face the lads. 'And fucking do it naked.'

'You fucking new boy!' someone else cried. 'Get in there!'

I knew this was a test, and a massive part of that test was showing zero fear. I removed my trainers, socks, T-shirt and trousers. When I was down to my underpants they all started clapping in time, 'Off! Off! Off!' And off they came. There was nothing to do but go for it and hope I wouldn't get one of those nasty daggers of glass slashing down my face or ripping into a major artery or, even worse, my nut sack. I didn't think. As the chants got louder I dived.

I felt a thumping hardness on my chest as I landed, then the sound of shattering glass and the slick and slide of beer on the polished floor. The cuts were painless. At first. I was just aware of the sensation of prickling and slicing and skin opening up. As I skidded forwards in the foaming beer river, I whipped my body around quickly, trying to angle my back and arse at the floor.

As I slid to the end, the slipstream pulled bunches of glass around my body. I pushed myself to my feet as carefully as I could without betraying the fact that I gave a shit. When I was up, Bus grabbed me in a headlock and started punching the crown of my skull. 'Welcome to the brotherhood!' he shouted. From my position under his armpit I could see the blood pouring down the pale skin of my arm, back and arse cheek. Other members of the Airborne began volunteering, diving into the glass themselves with maniacal cackling. Behind us, pool players continued with their game, showing a complete lack of interest in what was taking place.

I spent the whole of the next week picking glass out of my arse. But at least, I told myself, I was in the gang now. My pleasure at that fact would have been greater hadn't one of the older lads, who was probably jealous of the attention I'd been getting from Bus, reminded me as I paced back naked towards my clothes, 'But don't forget you're still a fucking sprog.'

That was the depressing thing about it all. I always wanted to be the best, but there was no way of climbing up this hierarchy by excellence. You needed to be in with the right people and you needed to have been in for a long time. The only way you could really earn rapid success in 9 Para was by your level of roguery. It was bad behaviour, more than any achievement or skill or experience in the field, that made someone feel they had the right to call themselves Airborne. Aside from that, you had to stay in the middle of the pack. You couldn't highlight yourself in front of Bus and the rest. If you did, you'd be smacked down, smartly and with prejudice.

What made it worse was that this was an era in which nothing much was going on in the world to keep the power-packs in the military occupied. Between 1998 and 2002 there were no deployments. There was no Afghanistan. There was no Iraq. The psychological machinery of the army is dedicated to the creation of a certain type of man, one who generates aggression. And that aggression needs an outlet. It needs a battlefield. It needs operations. In a war zone all that furious energy is incredibly effective. But without it, the men just turn it on each other. There's nowhere else for it to go.

As soon as I returned to the UK I had the wings tattooed on my left arm. Back in Aldershot I found myself in a bunk near Cranston. Now that I'd passed my initiation – and had learned my place – we were getting on better with each other. Every evening we'd all go drinking in local Airborne pubs and clubs like The Peggy or Cheeks. The lads would compete with each other to see who could dream up the most shocking behaviour. Some nights they'd be drinking pints of each other's piss. Other nights they'd be lowering their bollocks into the pockets of a pool table and having balls fired right at them, or taking their tops off and having darts throwing into their backs. 'Airborne!' would come the cry, as another act of debauchery went down. 'Airborne!' as the vomit ran. 'Airborne!' as the glass smashed. 'Airborne!' as pool ball smashed into nutsack. 'Airborne!' as we were chased by the military police all over town once again.

And me? I was swallowed right into it. I had to be. I wanted to be accepted. I wanted that sense of belonging. I wanted to be in that elite club. Acting like this was the only way to prove yourself and gain a little bit of status. If you didn't, they'd quickly pick up on it and make your life hell. I'd come a long way since I'd been that polite, young grammar-school lad, fresh off the ferry from Normandy, lifting his hat to everyone who passed him on the street and bidding them a cheery good morning.

I managed to avoid the violence until one night at Cheeks. We were all sitting in our usual place, having taken over several tables, and concentrating on the serious business of getting as pissed as we could as quickly as we could, beneath the glow-in-the-dark images of singers like Michael Jackson and Madonna on the walls around us, when the biggest lump of a man any of us had ever seen walked past. He was in a muscle vest and had more gold rings on his fingers than a gypsy fortune teller.

'Oi, Middleton,' leered Cranston. 'Go and hit him.'

'Fuck off,' I laughed.

Then Bus grinned at me from over the rim of his pint. 'Go on, Middleton,' he said. 'Hit him.'

There'd be no backing out of this now. As soon as Bus had issued his kingly decree, I was swamped with excited Paras, all of them shouting 'Airborne!', 'Airborne!', Airborne!' I staggered to my feet, trying to disguise not only how pissed I was but also how much I was shitting myself. By now the lump had found his mates, who had congregated around the jukebox.

'Airborne!', 'Airborne!', 'Airborne!'

There was nothing else I could do – and no point in drawing it out. I strode towards him. He saw me coming. His whole group turned. I knew I'd have to do it without hesitation, and do it properly. Anything less than a clean knockout and this animal would have me resembling the contents of a butcher's bin. I balled my fist, raised my arm and put the force of my entire body into it, squeezing my eyes shut at the force of knuckles on his jaw. A jolt of pain shot through the bones of my hand. Jesus Christ, the lump had barely moved. He was just looking back at me, slightly confused and irritated, as if by a fly. And then, he swung back. I somehow ducked it and, luckily, the lads were ready. They pounced on the poor guy and gave him a serious shoeing while I staggered back to the bar for another round of flaming sambucas.

Hours later we were on our way home, having taken over the whole top deck of the night bus. The few civilians that were forced to share the space with us were intimidated but pretending not to be, each one staring intently out of the window as the dark streets, silhouettes of terraced housing and glowing orange street lights bumped past. We were in our usual state, shouting, swearing, laughing and generally living up to our legendary reputations. It felt almost a duty in public. People had expectations of 9 Para, and nobody wanted to let them down. I'd had a brilliant night. Despite the fact that I'd failed to fell the big fella back at The Peggy, I knew my status had gone up a notch with everyone, and I took a secret pleasure in knowing that it had all been Cranston's idea. The last thing he would have wanted was for his suggestion to lead to Bus and the lads embracing me further into the fold, but you could just tell that that's what had happened. I felt elated.

As the bus swung round the corner towards the barracks I decided on a little stunt, just to cement this evening as mine in the minds of the boys. I staggered out of my seat, made my way to the front of the bus and turned around, holding onto the seats either side of me in an effort to keep upright.

'Oi, oi, oi!' I shouted, catching Bus's eye.

He looked back at me. 'Middleton!' he shouted. 'Miiiiiddddduuullllltooooooooon!!'

Everyone turned. I raised both arms triumphantly and shouted 'Airborne!' The cry immediately came back,

'Airborne!' And, as it did, I allowed my bursting bladder to release. Hot piss ran down my jeans, trickling into my socks and onto the floor of the bus, where it ran backwards in little streams. The lads erupted into cheers and laughter. Just as I was about to wobble back to my seat, I saw someone looking at me. She must have been in her fifties and I guessed, from the way she was dressed, that she was something like an office cleaner returning home from her night shift. She said, 'I bet your mum's proud of you.'

MY NEXT DEPLOYMENT was in August 2001. Operation Essential Harvest was a NATO mission in Macedonia, and the 'essential harvest' we had to assist in gathering was one of firearms. Macedonia was one of those troubled Balkan states that always seemed to be on the edge of some fresh conflict whose roots ran back into the distant past. We were there to collect weapons from rebel forces for destruction at a special site in Greece, thereby helping to prevent civil war. The Brits were the largest contingent there, with more than a thousand men from the Paras and the 2nd Battalion join-ing smaller numbers of French, Germans and Czechs. 9 Para were set up close to the mountains and we were billeted in a local hotel. Day to day, we were setting up checkpoints, making sure that communications were working and sitting behind desks in big tents, collecting weapons from fighters and logging serial numbers.

It was all pretty standard until I was selected to go and work with the French Foreign Legion. Word had got around that I spoke fluent French, and the next thing I knew I was interpreting for high-ranking officers from the Legion's Second Foreign Parachute Regiment, or 'Deuxième Rep'. They were an elite group that functioned a bit like the Special Forces. To say they operated in a different culture would be an understatement. These men were intelligent, as well as being trained to a level that would have left many Paras collapsed in a ditch. They behaved in a way that showed they had nothing to prove. Although Operation Essential Harvest was officially a dry tour, the Foreign Legion are actually sponsored by Kronenbourg. I was smuggling crates back to the Paras' hotel but drinking with the French. When they got wasted they didn't beat each other up. They sang old patriotic songs together like a bunch of merry pirates. I loved it. There were moments when I seriously considered packing it all in and joining the Legion. It was so good to be out of that violent bubble. I felt, for the first time in ages, properly accepted and respected. I was me again.

One morning I went into a hangar where the Paras used to eat and saw everyone was congregated in one corner. 'That's a bit weird,' I thought. I barged my way past a few people, before finding a crate on the floor by the wall. I stepped up onto it and peered over the heads. They were all transfixed by a portable TV, a big black box with a tiny screen and an aerial sticking out the top. An aeroplane was flying into a huge tower block somewhere. 'It's going to fucking kick off,' muttered someone. Nobody responded. They didn't have to.

Spending so much time with the Deuxième Rep had a powerful effect on me. It made me question what I'd been doing and who I'd become. I began to think, 'Is this who I am now? Is this what I'm going to have to do throughout my whole career? Is this who I aspire to be these days? Is my life's ambition to become the next Bus?' I'd allowed myself to become part of the crowd. I'd been sucked into it. And that's exactly what the military wants.

There are lots of important things about being part of a group. When it's working, it's about not putting yourself at the forefront of your thinking. It's about being dedicated to each other. Living and working together – and fighting and making up – turns you into a band of brothers. You might go through phases when you literally hate one another, but when the crunch comes you're so defensive on behalf of everyone in your group that you'd do anything to protect them. Concern for your own safety disappears and your only thought is for the safety of your brothers. And that is reciprocated.

It happened to me many times in Afghanistan. One day I was out on patrol when I saw a flatbed truck with a massive gun on the back of it driving past at the end of a dusty side street. We went to ground and watched it go. Suddenly it stopped. We quickly identified it as a 120mm anti-tank/ anti-aircraft weapon, a hugely valuable asset to the enemy. I turned to my officer and said, 'Let's not waste any time, let's go and secure it.' Before we knew it, we were up and sprinting towards it, zig-zagging between buildings, approaching with our weapons raised. Everyone else had been left behind.

Soon we found ourselves out in a clearing on the other side of a huge corn field. Two men in the truck saw us, leapt out of the cab and sprinted towards the field. My officer immediately launched himself after them. It would be incredibly dangerous in there, with no field of vision whatsoever and two armed Talibs on the loose in among the seven-foot corn. I thought to myself, 'I hope he's not going in there. He's the boss, we need him.' But he was. Without another thought I ran after him and shouted, 'Stay with the gun.' And then it was me in that corn field and him in the relative safety of the clearing. I remember thinking, 'What the fuck am I doing in here?' But it was an automatic reaction.

That is the power of the group at its best. But what marks a true leader out is the ability to separate yourself from those psychological forces when you need to. You can't allow group thinking to push you around too much. When I was young there was always something pulling me away from the crowd. It wasn't as if I was thinking, 'I want to lead.' It's just, looking back, I can see that it was in me. It's these people who can stand apart from crowds that the military seek for service in the Special Forces. They're taken out of the green army and put together in one elite group. The result is a gang of highly competitive men – a team of individuals. It's why they refer to them as the 'thinking soldiers'.

As deeply as I sank into the groupthink of 9 Para, somehow that respectable young man I'd once been was never quite killed off. My assignment with the Deuxième Rep had reawakened him, reminding me who I really was. From that point on I found myself gradually separating from Bus, Cranston and the rest.

What pulled me apart further still was the fact that, back in the UK, I'd met a girl. It happened when I was in Portsmouth visiting my nan. I'd gone for a drink in a club called Route 66 with a couple of old friends and was approached by a stylish woman with a blonde bob who told me her name was Hayley. Following some awkward flirting, we slept together. After that we just kind of slipped into a relationship. This didn't go down well with the lads from 9 Para. The first clue that the flock had decided to reject me was that the banter stopped. From the outside, the banter we used to indulge in could probably seem harsh, like bullying, but it was an integral part of the 9 Para world. It was a way of saying what you really thought about someone while turning it into a joke. Banter was always more than a bit of truth, however. It was also a test of your armour. If you couldn't take it, you'd get the shit ripped out of you.

But there was also something affectionate about it. You only shared banter with people you'd accepted as part of your group. In the Forces, it's when the banter stops that you're in trouble. And, with me, it stopped dead. 'Why are you not drinking down The Peggy?' they kept asking me. 'What's your fucking problem?' I'd come back from weekends in Portsmouth with Hayley to find my room trashed – my bed upside down, CDs smashed, locker door ripped off, clothes everywhere covered in piss and shit. I'd wake up in the middle of the night to see Cranston, Bus and three or four others just standing over me, staring at me, all of them pissed.

I'd find any excuse not to hang around with them. But as much as I wanted to get away, I just wasn't having a great deal of fun with Hayley. Despite this, I somehow found myself flying to Cancun and marrying her in a hotel, with her mum and friend watching. There was no great romantic scene, no bending down on one knee and proposing. Even as I was saying 'I do,' I was thinking, 'What the fuck have I got myself into?' A year later, with the relationship failing further, we decided that having a child might save us. The child was Oakley. He was born on 12 November 2001 in Frimley Park Hospital in Surrey. Although I love him dearly, and today we enjoy a fantastic relationship, he didn't save us.

But at least being married meant I could stay in married quarters, away from the others. By this time I was doing everything possible by myself – working out, running, eating. My attitude became 'Fuck you,' and that was interpreted as cockiness. And maybe I *was* cocky. I really was beginning to look down on them. To me they were nothing more than a bunch of pub soldiers, thirty-year-old infants with their ball-bags in a pool table. It was pathetic. Of course, they took every opportunity to throw my disrespect back at me. There was one day when I forgot to put a fire extinguisher back in its bracket and it went off in the back of a wagon. I was called to the office. The moment I walked in, someone jumped out from behind the door, grabbed me in a headlock and started digging me in the stomach. 'You need to start switching on,' they were saying. 'You're just going out there and doing your own thing. You're going to get yourself in fucking trouble.' He dropped me on the floor and I lay there, winded, thinking, 'You fucking cowards, grabbing me from behind.'

But at least it left me in no doubt. 9 Para. They weren't gods. They were dicks. The army wasn't what I thought it would be. They didn't care about excellence. They actually resented it. You weren't there to shine. You were there to know your place and stay in it. It came as no surprise to anyone when I finally knocked on the door of my sergeant and told him I wanted to leave.

'Why?' he asked.

'I just want to pursue a career elsewhere,' I said.

'Well, if you're sure,' he shrugged.

The truth was, I had no idea what I was going to do. Hayley and I were arguing constantly. I was spending more and more time alone, consumed with rage. And I didn't know whether I'd failed at the army or the army had failed me.

LEADERSHIP LESSONS

Stand apart from the crowd. You're a leader, not a follower. That's especially hard to remember when you first join any group, whether it be a military squadron or a corporation. There's an expectation, especially when you're new, that you'll 'join in' and become one of the gang. You need to hit that balance. If you completely separate yourself, you won't win trust. But never forget – if you have your sights set at the top, you need to resist coming across as just another dog in the pack.

Crowds are egotistical. Every group you'll ever belong to will tell themselves they're the best. As a leader, you need to let that myth flourish, because it creates motivation. But you should also be constantly on guard not to believe it yourself. I've seen many leaders fail because arrogance breeds complacency.

Humility means being open to inspiration. Keeping yourself humble also means you're able to identify exceptional people around you, who are better models of what you might one day be. I know that many of the lads in 9 Para would have dismissed the men from the Deuxième Rep as being boring and stuffy. In doing so, they'd have blinded themselves, missing an opportunity to lift themselves into a superior world.

MAKE FRIENDS WITH YOUR DEMONS

SOMETIMES IT'S ONLY by looking back that you can spot the moments when you made your biggest, most life-changing decisions. At the time, you're too much in the eye of the storm. The change seems too enormous. The unknown places that lie on the other side of it are too dark and frightening to contemplate. So you pretend it's not happening. You push it away, think about something else. You quietly decide to deal, another day, with the sudden understanding that you're so unhappy that, at some point soon, you're going to have to grab the steering wheel and yank your life in a radically new direction.

When I look back on it I realise it was in Macedonia that I first knew, deep down, that my days in the green army were numbered. In the civilised yet elite men of the Deuxième Rep I saw a different way of serving, a different way of fighting and a different way of achieving excellence. I glimpsed the possibility of a different future; a way of being me that was faithful to the truth of who, in my heart, I was. In the actual moment, though – as I joined in yet another round of merry,

Kronenbourg-fuelled French singing – all I knew was that the respect I had for my tribe of paratroopers was dying.

I'd love to tell you that, when I left 9 Para, I immediately transformed back into my cheery and gentle former self, but true stories are never that simple. Life makes you work harder than that. The fact is, I went the long way round. Not wanting to socialise with Bus and the others didn't alter the fact that, slowly but surely, I had become one of their kind. No matter how much I might have missed aspects of my younger self, I simply wasn't that innocent little boy any longer. I had been changed by my experiences. I was a man now. And, more than that, I was a paratrooper. I'd forgotten how to be anyone else. Getting back to the core of myself would be a long journey. Finally getting there would mean making friends with my demons. And before I could do that, I'd first have to find them and fight them.

I'd meet those demons on the streets of Portsmouth. Separating myself from 9 Para, and avoiding the endless rows with Hayley, meant spending as much time as possible with Nan, which meant being in the town where I'd grown up. This had an unexpected effect on me. I found myself thinking more and more about my real dad. Vivid and detailed memories of him would pop into my head out of nowhere, as if someone had switched on a TV.

He could hardly have been more different from my step-father. His name was Peter Aaron and he'd been a software engineer at IBM. Not only did he never lay a finger on me or my brothers, he barely even told us off. One of the long-forgotten scenes that appeared in my mind – and kept playing and replaying – took place just before he died. A friend named Simon from down the road had come round to play. Simon and I were passing the time, bumping down the stairs on our arses. After doing it a few times, Simon sat on the top step and decided he didn't want to go again. I didn't care, but he was blocking me. In a fit of temper I pushed him with my foot. Simon tumbled down the stairs, burst into tears and grassed me up in a loud wail. I thought, 'Uh oh, I'm in trouble here.' But when Dad came to see what had happened he just smiled up at me and said, 'Play nicely, lads.'

We moved to Australia when I was one and lived there for three years. I started to get flashbacks of that former life, too – a place of warmth and fun and unconditional love that was soon to vanish completely. I could see him in a swimming pool under a perfect blue sky, holding these two white kittens. I could see him teaching me to ride my bike. I could see him putting the seats down in the back of the car and making a bed with pillows before we went on a long journey. I could see him holding my hand as we walked to the shop to get chocolate digestives. He loved chocolate digestives and would literally eat them by the pack.

The more I thought about Dad, the angrier I became at the fact he'd been taken from me when I was so young. Following the strange and sudden events of his passing, our family gained a lot of money and lost everything that was important. It was only now I was a man that I realised how cruel it was that we hadn't been allowed to mourn him. As a child, you just accept things. Now that I was old enough to understand, I was sick with fury. The day after he'd died, every photo of him disappeared from the house. His smiling face vanished from walls, shelves and the front of the fridge. Me and my brothers were forbidden from talking about him, by threat of beating. We weren't even allowed to go to his funeral. His death was made absolute.

Dad's death might have caused the sky to rain money, but that didn't mean life was easy. My new stepfather loved us and sincerely tried to do his best for us, but he was from a completely different background and his values were alien to the ones Dad had raised us with. My stepfather had been raised tough. We got used to him returning from the pub with cuts and bruises and black eyes from fighting, and that would lead to screaming arguments with Mum. He thought me and my brothers were soft. He was determined to toughen us up. He was incredibly competitive by nature and always insisted his stepchildren had to be the absolute best at everything. My thing was football. There might have been nothing to me, size-wise, but I could run fast and had stamina. I had a bit of talent, too. I'd been on Southampton's books from the age of seven and also played in my local side. My stepfather was our coach. He'd turn up to games in a knee-length leather raincoat, cycling shorts and black boots, with a Rottweiler at the end of a leash.

If he looked like a lunatic, he could act like one as well. Before every match he'd storm into the changing room with his dog and blare out 'Simply the Best' by Tina Turner at top volume on a ghetto blaster. He'd make us all play in shirts that he'd sent to the printers to have 'SIMPLY THE BEST' stamped across the back. The other parents were petrified of him. One goalkeeper who came to play with us was just brilliant, but his father ended up removing him after one season because our team was so ultra-competitive. I started hating going to football because of the pressure he put on me. I always had to be the best, to play at my very highest capacity. The only way I knew I'd be OK, and stay out of trouble, was by being out in front of everyone else. To win was to be safe.

At home he ruled with an iron fist. When we moved to France he insisted that our big house was kept spotless at all times. I could never have friends round because I knew after dinner he'd make us spend literally an hour and a half cleaning up – scrubbing pots and mopping floors. I'd do everything in my power to keep him on his good side, because his bad side was frightening. He'd punish us physically, sometimes badly, with a belt or a wooden spoon or his open hands, with me curled up in the corner of the room. A part of me thinks I got the brunt of things because I looked so much like my real dad and, so I'm told, acted like him too.

The only place I didn't feel the need to excel was at school. It wasn't that I was badly behaved. I was captain of the athletics team and the football team, and all the teachers liked me. I would never have dared be cheeky. The problem was, I just didn't have much interest in learning and I could never seem to concentrate. I was at my happiest when I was reading my *SAS Survival Book* and playing with my brothers on our large patch of family land, which even had its own woodland. We had so much space, we were like little gypsy kids, hunting and scrambling around, playing with Rambo knives and bows and arrows.

One summer, when I was ten, my stepfather bought us all air rifles. At the end of a long, fun day I was out with my elder brother Michael when I saw a grey squirrel running up the trunk of a tall pine tree. Without thinking, I aimed and fired. It fell out of the tree, making a horrible cracking sound as it hit the branches on its way down, and landed in a bed of dry pine needles at our feet.

'You idiot,' said Michael.

'What shall we do?' I asked. It was staring up at me with its little black eyes.

'Nothing,' he said. 'Leave it.'

'Do you think it'll be all right?'

We stared at it for a moment. It was bleeding from its backside where I'd shot it. Its arms were twitching.

'Yeah,' said my brother. 'Maybe.'

When we got back to the house we told my stepfather what had happened. He was standing in the huge doorway of our house.

'And it's still alive?' he said, looming over us. 'That's what you're telling me?'

'I think so,' I said.

'If you're old enough to shoot it, you're old enough to kill it,' he said. 'Get back there and finish it off.'

We returned to the woodland as slowly as we could in the hope its heart would have given out by the time we reached it. It was in a terrible state when we found it. Blood was matted in its fur and its tiny pink mouth was moving. Michael didn't say anything as I raised the barrel of the air rifle. My hands were trembling, which was making the rifle move. Worried I would miss again, I pushed the muzzle up against the squirrel's little head, closed my eyes and pulled the trigger. There was a dull thud.

'Shit,' said Michael. 'You did it.'

Walking back towards the house, I was too dazed with guilt and remorse to really speak. Of course, I could never have imagined it would one day be my job to do the same thing to grown men. I'd sometimes think of that squirrel when I was raising my weapon to fire. I felt worse for that animal than I would for any of them.

It was a retired major, whose house was being renovated by my stepdad, who first suggested I might have what it takes to succeed in the military. 'You're a good worker and you're fit,' he'd said. 'You'd have a good career.' By that stage I was sick of school. All I wanted to do was run around outside in the mud, making camps and shooting targets. The idea of being paid to do that sounded pretty good, and the fact that I'd get to leave home was a major bonus.

And now, here I was, a fully-fledged member of 9 Parachute Squadron. And I'd come to hate it. One afternoon, a few weeks after my return from Macedonia, we were returning in a military wagon from an exercise when we passed a road sign that said Wood Green. I hadn't seen or heard those two words in years. Sitting in the back of that noisy wagon, I felt swamped by a thousand long-lost childhood memories. I saw a row of smart brick semi-detached houses. I saw a sweet shop. I saw a park that I used to explore that had a massive, make-shift spiderweb that I used to love climbing. I saw a red postbox outside my granddad's house. I saw myself standing beside it with my eyes squeezed tightly shut, counting to one hundred, during a game of hide and seek with my beloved Uncle Tony, who was only ten years older than me.

'You all right?' asked the guy sitting next to me, a decent Scottish lad named Greg.

'Wood Green,' I said. 'It's where my dad's family lives. My real dad. I've got uncles and aunties there. Haven't seen them in, like, years.'

'Not seen them?'

'Yeah, it was my mum,' I said. 'She wouldn't allow it, so we lost touch. Shame, really.'

'You should go and visit,' he said. 'Your mam cannae stop you now.'

'I wouldn't have a clue how to find them,' I said, as the military wagon sped further and further away. 'It was a long time ago. Too long, really.'

The following evening Greg and I went out for a couple of beers. I'd had yet another row with Hayley, and felt a sudden and overwhelming need to get drunk. Everything was going wrong. Anger was circling me like so many birds of prey. I was angry at the army, I was angry at Cranston and Bus, and I was angry at all the cowardly arseholes who'd jumped me the week before. I was angry at my wife. I was angry at my mum for stealing my dad's memory from me. I was angry at the knowledge that I had family out there that I'd been forbidden from seeing and who were now completely lost. I was angry that the boy I'd once been had been changed into a man I didn't like or even recognise.

At somewhere near closing time I went for my final piss of the night. Staggering out of the bathroom, I saw that Greg had moved onto the dance floor. And it looked like someone was getting up in his face. As I pushed my way through the crowd towards him, the moving bodies seemed to part of their own volition. I was in a dark tunnel, and all I could see at the end of it was a twenty-year-old knobhead in a white Adidas top shoving my mate with the heels of his hands.

All of the rage I'd felt over the last few months entered my fist and exited, explosively, into his chin. He flew back about six feet and fell sprawling onto the floor. The crowd opened up around him in horror. He didn't move. I'd knocked him out with one punch. It felt good. It felt amazing. In that moment I decided the nice boy from Normandy was dead. If anybody gave me any shit from now on, they were going to get their jaw broken.

WHEN YOU LEAVE the army you spend your final three months working on your 'resettlement package'. This means you're free to pursue the next phase of your life, whatever that might be. For the lack of any better idea I'd applied to join the Metropolitan Police Force and began a training course up at Hendon in north London. The most difficult thing about it was the culture shock. The rules of banter that operated in the social world of the Paras did not apply there. In my first week, at lunch, I sat down next to a guy who was wearing a turban with a police cap badge on it. I'd never seen anything like it.

'Fucking hell,' I said. 'I bet you get loads of shit for wearing that on your head.'

I was expecting that to be the beginning of a conversation that would be interesting, honest and, most of all, bonding. In the army he would have come back with a joke about it, like, 'Yeah, it's the craphat of all craphats' – something of that sort. But that wasn't what happened. He reacted badly.

'Well, no, I wear this because of my religion,' he said.

The guy sitting opposite me looked disgusted. 'Ant, you just can't say things like that.' He picked up his tray and walked off.

I ate alone, confused and angry. I was only trying to start a conversation but had been made to feel like a racist arsehole.

On a day off from my course at Hendon I decided to drive to Wood Green. I thought I might bump into a member of my real dad's family or spot a familiar landmark. I suspected it would be a pointless mission, and that's exactly how it turned out. I spent two hours driving around, hoping to catch a glimpse of the red letter box that sat outside my granddad's house. It was ridiculous. I was on the way back to the barracks in Aldershot when, stuck in a long queue at some roadworks, I glanced a little way down a side road and spotted a phone box. It gave me an idea.

I pulled up beside it, slotted in a 20p and dialled my nan. She was my only hope, and a pretty desperate one – she was my mum's mum, so I knew it was highly unlikely she'd give up an address, even if she had one. If my mother found out I was even looking for dad's family, she'd go feral. I didn't even want to think how my stepfather might react. But what else could I do?

'How are you, Ant?' she said. 'How's the police?'

My credit jumped down suddenly on the little display on the phone. I decided to cut straight to it.

'I'm in Wood Green, Nan.'

There was a silence.

'And what are you doing in Wood Green, love?'

'Don't know,' I said. 'Just trying to find my aunty and uncles.'

'You know, your mum would be very upset if she knew,' she said.

'Yeah, I know that,' I said. 'But I'm my own man, now. I want to find them. It can't do any harm.'

'You'll break her heart.'

'By why, Nan? Why does it make any difference? My dad's my dad. Nothing's going to change that.' The static crackled down the phone line. 'She wouldn't even let us keep a photo of him.'

'She was only doing what she thought was best,' Nan replied. 'Why have all those painful memories hanging around the house?'

'But all I want to do is find out about him. What's wrong with that? I only want to know what he was like.'

Raindrops started to patter on the glass of the phone box.

'Nan?' I said.

She replied with a whisper. 'Risley Avenue.'

Then the phone went dead.

Risley Avenue! Of course! I recognised the name immediately. I raced into a newsagent's, got directions from the guy behind the counter and ten minutes later was turning into the street. Through my left-hand window there were rows of traditional red-brick terraces, but the houses on my side were much more distinctive, with many of the terraces being joined by unusual triangle shapes that housed the upstairs windows. I could remember looking at them with great curiosity, sitting in the back of the car when I was a kid.

This, I knew without doubt, was the street where my granddad lived. He'd been a tailor, and me and my brothers had been extremely close to him, even sometimes being allowed to see him for weekends after my dad passed away, before the move to France. When he was dying he'd asked to see us at his bedside so he could say a final goodbye. But we'd not been allowed. I was fourteen when he died. My Uncle Tony offered to pay for flights so we could come to his funeral. Mum, once again, refused.

As I drove further down Risley Avenue it all kept flooding back. It was almost too much. I remembered running to the shops to get sweets – I could remember the exact route. And down there was the way to the park with the fountain and the massive spiderweb. Although Granddad was no longer alive, his ex-partner used to live just a couple of doors away from him. We called her Nanny Ball. I could only pray that she was still alive and hadn't been moved into a care home or something.

I parked up and walked down the road, looking for her house. My heart leapt when I saw the hide-and-seek post box. It was right on the corner of a crossroads that had a small roundabout at its centre. And there was Granddad's old house. It was strange to see the place where I'd felt such happiness occupied by someone else, with a dilapidated plastic tractor abandoned on the front-yard lawn and a fat ginger cat staring territorially at me from the side passage. It was like seeing a stranger wearing your best trousers.

I walked on to Nanny Ball's place. I was thrilled to see that it didn't look changed at all, with its neat rows of flowers in the beds and the little stone statue of a boy holding a bird bath. I tried to contain my feelings as I gave the knocker a firm rap. Eventually someone came to the door. But my heart sank as it opened to reveal a six-foot-two biker with a huge grey beard and an AC/DC T-shirt.

'I'm sorry to disturb you, but I'm looking …'

He was smiling at me strangely. 'I know,' he said. 'I know exactly who you're looking for.'

'You do?'

'I think so,' he said. 'You don't know me, but I know you. It's Anthony, isn't it? Follow me.'

He disappeared for a moment to fetch his slippers, and then I followed him up the road. We arrived at a mid-terrace house with a hedge-covered fence and a grey gate. I rang the bell and stood back as the faint sound of footsteps grew louder and the door opened. There was a woman standing there. A woman that I hadn't seen for a very long time.

'Oh my God,' she said. 'Oh Jesus, I can hardly speak. Anthony! Anthony! I can't believe it's you!'

She put her hand over her mouth and burst into tears. I could barely speak myself.

'Hello, Auntie Maria.'

She led me next door, to where yet more members of my family were living. There I found a person I recognised instantly from some of my happiest memories. I've never seen such shock and joy on a person's face. He immediately embraced me, all three of us now crying. It was Uncle Tony.

'I haven't seen you since you were bloody seven years old,' he said. 'I've been praying for this day. We all have. Anthony, mate. I can't believe you've come.'

When we finally put each other down, I settled myself on the floor, crossing my legs, as I used to when I was a boy.

'You know, my brother – your dad – used to sit exactly like that,' said Tony, eyes brimming. 'He'd never sit on the settee. He'd just go crossed-legged on the rug like a little kid watching telly, even when he was bloody thirty. And he used to walk on his toes like you do. And the way you lift your eyebrows when you talk, Anthony. That's just like him. He had that caterpillar eyebrow, too.'

I made a mental note: the monobrow clearly needed some attention.

'It's incredible,' Tony continued. 'It really is. It's like my brother's come back to life.'

As the afternoon fled by I told him everything I remembered of Dad – the bedtime stories he'd read every night, and the pillow and quilt he'd spread out in the back of his car, and the kittens in the swimming pool in Australia. Tony couldn't believe how much I remembered, considering I was so young when Dad passed away. I found out lots I didn't know about Dad too, like he was a black belt in karate, he played rugby and supported Manchester United, and how his computer job took him all around the world, to places like America, South Africa and Canada.

But by the end of the afternoon both the sky outside and the mood inside had grown dark. For too long, my uncle and aunty had lived with the fury of Mum preventing us from seeing them. They were even angrier about her attempts at erasing Dad from our memory.

'It's as good as murder,' Uncle Tony said. 'She was trying to kill that poor man in the minds of his own children.'

'Don't ever believe he's not in my mind,' I said, my eyes getting wet again. 'I think about him every single day.'

We talked about it for hours. By the time I left, I'd gone from tearful elation to utter sorrow to vengeful rage. I felt about ready to kill someone.

The next time I saw my stepfather was when he came to Aldershot to pick me up, on my last day in the army.

'Thought I'd surprise you,' he said, leaning over to open the passenger seat. 'You can stay with us while you sort yourself out.'

'I'm not going with you,' I said.

'You what?' he said, scowling.

'I said I'm not going,' I said. 'I'm going to live with my uncle.'

'Your uncle?' he said, his eyes draining. 'And that's that what you want, is it?'

'That's what I want.'

He went silent for a moment, as the shock entered him. Then he punched the windscreen of the car.

'Get in this car,' he said. 'Get in this fucking car now.'

I picked up my bag and walked away.

WITH MY MOOD as it was, my relationship with Hayley was only becoming worse. I began dividing my time between Uncle Tony's house and a place in Hendon where the Met course took place. During the day I was learning about the law, role-playing potentially difficult scenarios, doing riot control. Having already been through the army system made the physical side of it a breeze. One thing I found strange, though, was that nobody at Hendon seemed to have heard of 9 Para. Whenever I'd mention them to anyone, they'd just look slightly blank. There was one guy in particular who I instantly bonded with, called Johnny. He happened to be a bit of an armchair expert on the military, having once harboured dreams of joining the Forces.

'I was a paratrooper,' I told him proudly, when we'd first chatted in the bar at Hendon after a particularly boring afternoon learning about the various definitions of theft.

'Airborne?' he said, eyes widening. 'Fuckin' 'ell! Sweet!' He narrowed his eyes. 'What regiment? One? Two? Three?'

I smiled proudly and sat back on my stool, bracing myself for his awestruck disbelief and his demands for tales of the legendary 9 Para debauchery. 'Nine,' I said.

'9 Para?' he said. 'What's 9 Para?'

'9 Parachute Squadron Royal Engineers. You know, 9 Para. *9 Para!* How the fuck can you not know 9 Para?'

'Is it part of the TA?'

It took a few experiences like this for me to finally realise that I'd been lied to. 9 Para weren't famous. They weren't legends. They were delusional. But that didn't stop me behaving like a cliched, horrible paratrooper. The strange thing was, now I wasn't in the Forces anymore I began cleaving to my old persona more than I'd ever done. It didn't matter that I'd totally rejected it when I'd been there – I'd wear my Para shirt at the gym, and use any opportunity to show off the tattooed wings on my left shoulder and to chug pints and shout 'Airborne!'

Walking away from the Paras meant walking away from the identity that the squadron had created for me. Now it was gone, I wasn't sure who I was. I certainly wasn't the young man who'd joined the services. The only thing I had to fall back on was that I was this 9 Para guy. People would say, 'Who are you?' and I'd reply, 'I'm ex-9 Parachute Squadron.' It was how I defined myself. But as soon as they heard that, I felt there was an expectation. In order to prove I was a Para I'd have to fulfil it or risk them thinking, 'You're not the person you said you were.' Ex-9 Parachute Squadron might not have been much of an identity, but it was the only one I had.

So the debauchery and destruction continued, and my new mate Johnny was only too happy to assist. While everyone else was revising for the course exams we'd go out on the piss and come back to the accommodation, wrap ourselves in toilet paper like mummies and smash the place up. The lack of revision I was doing turned out not to be too much of an obstacle, as I'd also made friends with a left-handed genius called Greg. I made sure I sat next to him in the exam hall so he could slide his paper across for me to see. Needless to say, I aced every test.

It wasn't long before the inevitable happened and Hayley and I decided to split. Try as we might, the marriage just wasn't working and we thought it best to go our separate ways.

When I discovered that more members of my dad's extended family lived up in Chelmsford I started hanging out there, too. Once I'd formally split with Hayley I moved there permanently. Up in Essex I found myself drawing a lot of unwanted attention. The problem was, I was confident, in good physical shape and the girls seemed to like me. And I liked them right back. I began bulking myself up with the help of regular sessions in the gym and steroids that I'd score from a lad I'd come to know locally. I found that a certain type didn't appreciate people like me in their vicinity. I was too much of a threat.

I never looked for trouble, but when it found me I wouldn't hesitate. There was no in between. I was like a switch: if I was on, whoever was facing up to me would be knocked out – I'd fucking annihilate him until he stopped moving. I quickly learned that if I aimed my knuckle at just the right part of the chin, I could knock anyone out and leave them with a broken jaw as a parting gift. People began to joke, 'I've never seen Ant in a fight,' because there never was one. Whatever someone started, I'd stop in under three seconds. And I did a lot of stopping. It's true what they say about steroids. What you gain in muscle mass you lose in control over your temper. It's a dangerous, stupid trade-off, and one I should never have made. I have Emilie, my future wife, to thank for persuading me to stop taking them.

Two weeks before the end of my four-month Met course I went out for a boozy Saturday with Johnny in Southampton. We were leaving a club called Oceana at about 2 a.m. and I asked him to chuck me the keys. I'd always drink-drive, and felt that alcohol didn't really have much of a debilitating effect on me. In the army I'd grown well used to drinking until 4 a.m. and then being up two hours later for an eight-mile run. I jumped behind the wheel of Johnny's little red Vauxhall Vectra and decided to take a shortcut down a one-way street. I was halfway down it when the entire street started flashing blue. Shit. Police.

I was twice over the limit. They arrested me and locked me in a freezing cell. As I sat on the edge of the mattress, staring at the concrete floor, I knew this would be the end of my attempted career as a police officer. But I didn't have a long dark night of the soul. I had a nice kip.

The fact is, I didn't care. What with the failure of my army career, the failure of my marriage, the grief Hayley was giving me, the estrangement from my mother's family and all the turmoil in my head about Dad, my life and existence had started to mean nothing to me. Sure enough, I was kicked out of Hendon on the Monday and was drink-driving again by Tuesday. I was even caught a second time, earning myself a two-year ban in the process. Who cared? If I ended up in prison, nobody would miss me.

My relationship with my dad's family was also now causing me pain. I was seeing a lot of my Uncle Tony, and his talk about Dad and what happened to him was becoming so relentless and intense I felt it was bordering on obsessive. At first I'd been proud when he'd tell me how similar I was to him, but it was now overwhelming. Because my nan was in an awkward situation, I didn't talk about Uncle Tony and the others with her. So I was amazed when, one Saturday afternoon, just as I was leaving her place after dinner, she said, 'I'll take you down the grave if you want.'

'Would you? Dad's grave?'

'If you want.'

We made the journey a week later. It turns out he was buried in a little back-street church in a pretty tea-and-scones village in Hampshire called Hambledon. We stopped at a florist's on the way to pick up some flowers. When we arrived, Nan stayed back and pointed me in the right direction. It was a lonely, gusty day and the only sound in the place was the wind in the tall elms. I approached it slowly, not quite sure how I was going to handle it. The small headstone was at the back of the plot, near an old, crumbling wall, and the gold writing on it was already almost completely worn away. It just said: PETER AARON, LOVING FATHER AND HUSBAND. I put the flowers down and collapsed, tears pouring down my face, my sobs getting lost in the roaring of the wind as it barrelled angrily around the graveyard.

That night I drove back to my new flat in Chelmsford, which had a balcony overlooking a car park. I'd only recently moved in and had invited some of my new Essex mates around to see it. We were all out on the balcony, drinking champagne, when three young guys walked past. One of them shouted, 'Fucking hell, nice view!' The switch flipped. I ran downstairs, chased one of them for about ten yards, got him in a headlock and started swinging at his head.

'How dare you?' I shouted at him. 'I'm having a nice time up there with my friends' – *punch* – 'I'm not disturbing you' – *punch* – 'I'm a nice' – *punch* – 'polite' – *punch* – 'respectful person' – *punch, punch, punch*. 'And yet you shout at me.' *Punch*. My fist was wet with blood and snot. It was disgusting, and only made me angrier. 'There's no way I'd be so rude as to shout "nice view" at someone.' *Punch*. 'So why shout it at me?' *Punch*. 'You're going to think twice about walking past someone's balcony and saying "Nice view."'

It was only when I realised he was unconscious that I dropped him.

When I woke up the next morning I was alone. I remembered, vaguely, going to a club after the party. I tried to work out what had happened next. I'd obviously lost my keys and booted the door in. It was completely off its hinges, split in half with a big bootprint on it. And I was covered in blood, even though I wasn't injured.

A couple of weeks later, word reached me that the police were trying to track me down. At first I assumed I was wanted for questioning over the guy in the car park. It turned out to be someone else – a known face around Chelmsford who I knew didn't like me. He was the kind of character who got beaten up regularly, and he'd told the police I'd bitten a chunk out of his cheek. I hadn't done that, but it was my word against his, and by now I had a reputation. The police were determined to have me locked up, whatever the truth of the matter. Innocent or not, the police had a knack for getting their way. I knew there was at least a 70–30 chance I'd be locked up for six to eight years. There was only one person in the world I could talk to about this. I bought two litres of whisky, got in my car and drove all the way to Hampshire. I drank the liquor and wept, then slept the night on my dad's grave.

In order to avoid the police I moved into my mate's house, above a garage, and made an arrangement to get a fake passport. The plan was to escape to Australia, to lie low for a while. A few days before my meeting with the passport guy I went for a drink with my cousin Terry at a pub called the Ivory Peg in Chelmsford. We'd just rocked up to the bar when Terry jabbed me in the ribs.

'Hey, that's Emilie Dines.'

'Is it?' I said, craning my neck to look at the girl behind the bar.

Emilie Dines was about as notorious around Chelmsford as I was, except she was famous for her incredible beauty. Of course, Essex is crammed with people who think they're beautiful but, for once, I could see this woman's legend was well deserved. She had browny-green eyes, and wore a tight white shirt and her long dark hair in a ponytail. Her figure was unbelievable, the kind of body you dream about but somehow never think exists in real life.

'Hi Emilie,' said Terry, trying to act casual, when it was our turn to get served. 'Have you met Ant?'

'All right?' she said to me, her eyes barely shifting in my direction.

'Hello,' I said. 'How you doing?'

'Great, yeah,' she said, before turning away to deal with our drink.

'She's going out with a copper,' Terry whispered.

A few nights later, Terry and I were in a pub called The

Toad. It was during Euro 2004 and we were waiting to watch England–Croatia. And there was Emilie, sitting among her girlfriends, in a yellow and white flower-print dress. I found myself just gazing stupidly at her. To my amazement she turned and beamed back at me, budging up on the bench so I could sit.

'How you been?' I said.

And, just like that, we were talking. And we didn't stop. The game that I'd been looking forward to watching all week became just a smear of background noise. I felt complete, somehow, as if in Emilie I was seeing all the beauty I'd ever need to see.

At one point in the evening I asked her, 'What do you want out of life?'

She smiled again and said, 'I just want to have fun, really.'

There was something about the way she said the word 'fun' that gave me a suspicion she might like me. Still, she had a boyfriend, and that boyfriend was a policeman. I forced myself to say my goodbyes and went on my way. I had to meet a man about a passport.

I tried to forget her, I really did. But I didn't do a very good job. About a week later I was up to my arse in grease, working for cash in my mate's car workshop, when my Nokia buzzed. It was Emilie, a text message. REALLY GOOD TO CHAT THE OTHER NIGHT. NOW YOU HAVE MY NUMBER. Because my phone had no credit, I couldn't reply. But when I did finally call her, two days later, she told me that about half an hour after I'd left her the other night, she'd called up her boyfriend and told him it was over.

I suggested a date at a pretty village pub in Danbury called The Anchor. I picked her up in a 'borrowed' – a customer's silver Peugeot 206 from the workshop I'd been working in. Once again, we chatted all night. I was desperate not to mess this up, so decided to be upfront about all the reasons why she might decide I was a bad bet. There was a lot to say. I told her about the army. I told her about my first marriage. I told her about the police being after me. I told her about my plan with the fake passport and my escape to Australia. She listened, never seeming to judge, but never quite giving away what she thought. When we walked to the car, under the moonlight, she thanked me for dinner.

'You know what I think?' she said, leaning against the passenger door. 'You should go to the police. Hand yourself in.'

'I can't,' I said. 'I'm looking at eight years.'

'But you're innocent. And if they convict you, I'll wait. I want to be with you.'

'You wouldn't wait eight years,' I said.

'I know this sounds cheesy,' she said, 'but I've never felt like this about anyone before. The first time I saw you at the pub I told my best mate, "I love that guy." I can't actually believe I'm here with you.'

It was hard to take in what she was saying. Love? I felt like I was being offered the most incredible gift, but also the knowledge that I could never really have it – at least not if I went to the police.

'I'll tell you what,' I said. 'I'll get you a passport too. We can both go. It'll be fun.'

'Look how successful you were,' she said. 'You were a paratrooper, Ant. And look at you now. Do you remember, when we first met you asked me what I wanted? Well, what do *you* want? Don't you want to get the old Anthony back? That young lad you were telling me about. He seemed like a decent guy.'

'What am I supposed to do? I'm never going back to the army.'

'Is that the only choice?'

'Well, there is something else I've been thinking about, but ...'

'What is it?' she said. 'Tell me.'

'It's the Royal Marines. But ...'

And I couldn't say anything else, because she'd pulled me to her body and was kissing me.

The next day, at Chelmsford Police Station, I was charged with grievous bodily harm with intent, which is one down from manslaughter. The investigators seemed genuinely convinced I was guilty, and for that I can't really blame them. When you considered my reputation and the circumstantial evidence, which even I could see looked pretty bad, I'd have probably wanted to lock me up too.

On the day of the trial my accuser made two critical misjudgements. His first was climbing into the witness box caked in cheap foundation, his second was forgetting to charge up his brain cell before he came to court. My brilliant solicitor began her cross-examination by casually asking if his make-up might be disguising a black eye.

'Er, yep,' he said.

'And how did you get this black eye?'

'It was a fight. It wasn't nothing to do with me.'

'So why did you consider it necessary to cover it up?'

He grinned stupidly. 'It's not good for court, is it, a black eye?'

'So would it be fair to say that it was your intention to mislead the jury?'

He thought for a moment. 'Yeah, I guess.'

And that was it. It was his word against mine, and his word had just been proven in a court of law to be shit.

Case dismissed.

THERE WERE TWO different kinds of people on the train that pulled out of Exeter St Davids at 8.30 on that bright morning in March 2005: your ordinary commuters, zoned out in preparation for another dull day in the office, and the young men, pale and terrified and smartly dressed, with one-way tickets in their pockets. These lads would be getting off at Lympstone Commando, the station in the middle of nowhere that serves just one place: the legendary Royal Marines Commando Training Centre in Devon.

There were about thirty of us that tipped out onto the narrow concrete platform that day, wearing the suits we'd been instructed to arrive in. As the doors beeped and closed and the train eased off, we were hit by the cold wind coming off the bleak, muddy sands of the River Exe that stretched into the distance. In front of us were a high fence, a locked gate and a drill instructor.

'Intake 898!' he barked. 'Single file! Follow me!'

He marched us through the gate and up a long path that wound up a steep hill towards the barracks. We strode past a gigantic assault course through which a group of new recruits were grunting and gurning, their faces muddy, their breath rising in ghostly billows. I passed them hungry with anticipation, noting to myself once more how lucky I was to be there.

Justice had been done back in Chelmsford, but there was no way I was going to be complacent. I knew Emilie was right. I had to change. I had to take on my demons or I was going to end up in prison, no doubt about it. Leaving Essex would be a start. I used to see old guys in their fifties out there who were still fighting, and I knew that would be my fate if I didn't do something drastic. This meant finding a place that would pull something different out of me. It also meant making the most of this run of luck: things were going well with my relationship with Emilie, I was off the steroids and I'd also put my uncles and aunties at a distance, not because I didn't love them, but just because I was finding all the constant talk about my dad just too intense. The Royal Marines would be a new start. I felt both lucky and privileged to be able to make it.

It didn't take long for me to realise that I had found exactly the right place. Our new intake were returning to our accommodation after lunch when the drill sergeant came out into the corridor and called for me.

'Middleton!' he said.

I approached him with my heart sinking. How had I high-lighted myself already? Was this going to be a repeat of Pre-Para?

'Yes, Sergeant?' I asked.

'You were in the army, were you not?'

'Yes, Sergeant,' I said.

'P Company?'

'Yes, Sergeant.'

'Well, make sure you get your wings sewn onto your uniform.'

'Yes, Sergeant.'

It was, no doubt, an insignificant moment to my drill sergeant. To me it was everything. That little gesture of respect showed me that, unlike the army, the Royal Marines didn't respond to individual achievement with envy. They welcomed it. I wasn't going to be kicked into a ditch at Lympstone for the crime of coming first. Any strength they saw in you, they'd nurture. Although there were some guys in our intake who were edging thirty, most were nineteen or twenty. I was twenty-four, and having my wings stitched onto my kit earned me everyone's respect.

Trainees on the thirty-two-week course are known as 'nods', because they're run ragged and then pulled into class for lessons, during which it's not unusual to see them nodding off. The very newest intake wore orange ribbons to denote their status. I lost count of the number of double-takes I saw, from people clocking my orange ribbon and then the wings on my shoulder. It was a fantastic feeling, and couldn't have been more different from my time as a hated craphat.

I'd retained most of the weight I'd put on over the many hundreds of hours I'd put in at the gym, and I found the physical training to be punishing but fun. We were doing ten-mile marches with heavy weights, assault courses, rope climbs. The big revelation came in the classroom. In the Paras we'd only been taught dribs and drabs of fieldcraft, but the Commando course was another world. It was like going from kindergarten to Cambridge University. We were learning pure soldiering: battlefield patrolling, live firing, survival techniques, troop attacks, section attacks, map reading, judging distance. I'd had no idea how little I'd known when I was at Aldershot. I could run twenty miles back then, and down a pint and throw a punch, and that was it. I was becoming a true soldier and I was loving every minute of it.

On week fifteen us nods were finally allowed out for a drink, strictly between the hours of 18:00 and 23:00. I'd made friends with this big South African guy named Daniel, and we decided to get the train down to Exeter for our first beers in months. We had a brilliant evening, during which I told him all about Emilie, Oakley and my misadventures with 9 Para. We were walking back to Exeter St Davids when this guy, rushing for the train, barged past us, knocking me on the shoulder.

It took a fraction of a second, probably less. The switch switched. My fist went out and he was on the ground, mouth open, eyes gaping, not a muscle moving. The next thing I knew I was handcuffed and being bundled into the back of a police van. I couldn't believe what I'd done. This was it. 'I've lost my career,' I thought, as the van door slammed shut, leaving me in the unforgiving steel darkness. Somehow I was going to have to tell Emilie that, after all the faith she'd put in me, I was going to have to get my job back at the garage in Chelmsford.

When the police officers realised I was a new recruit they had me driven back to Lympstone for my superiors to deal with. The next morning I was pulled in to see the troop commander, an old-school type who'd worked his way up the ranks over the course of twenty years. He was a rangy man with dark eyes and a thick vein running down his fore-head, and was sitting at his desk with a pile of forms and files in front of him.

'Middleton,' he said. 'I can't have my men assaulting people in the streets. No ifs nor buts nor maybes. I just can't allow that to happen, it's as simple as that. If you can't control yourself, you have no place here. We don't want men who are unpredictable. We've no use for them.'

'Yes, sir,' I said.

'So if you don't want to end up in civvies, I suggest you get that head screwed on. Do you understand? I expect a man with your background to be setting an example.'

'Yes, sir,' I said.

He spoke slowly and looked me in the eye. 'Be a shepherd, not a fucking sheep.'

I hadn't felt this way since I was five years old, when Dad had forgiven me for kicking Simon down the stairs. From that point on I became resolute. That was it. Never again. I made an absolute vow to try to be deserving of the respect that the Royal Marines were giving me. That would mean fighting my demons. We all have dark forces living within us. They're part of being human. But they feed on damage. The more pain and injustice we go through in life, the stronger our demons become. Mine had been with me since I was five, but it had taken that pile-up of failures and the meeting with my dad's family to draw them out. And how low they'd taken me. Nearly to prison, and to a life of shame and blood.

I couldn't let them win anymore. I'd rein in the drinking. And I'd begin using every spare moment seeing Emilie. If I was given twelve hours off, I'd take the four-hour train service to Chelmsford, spend three hours with her, and return. After a few weeks of this my confidence began to blossom. I'd never felt more at home, or more accepted, just for being who I wanted to be.

The difference was stark. Every tribe has its own internal rules. In 9 Para you gained status by showing how many pints you could drink, how many fights you could get into and how much shock you could inspire in everyone at the next horrendous act you dreamt up. In the Marines you gained status through hard work. In 9 Para, and the wider green army, they were always pushing at your weaknesses and trying to bring you back down. The Marines were about building on your strengths, talking positively about each other, building each other up. The typical conversations you'd overhear around Lympstone would be like, 'He might be weak at this but he's fucking good at that.' I'd found my tribe, and I was thriving.

Around halfway through my Commando training a sniper course began. I was standing at the armoury on the first day when I became aware of an electric charge of excitement crackling through the air. Out of the door in front of us came a huge, broad-shouldered man wearing a green beret with a distinctive emblem that showed a raised dagger and two horizontal stripes, adorned with the motto BY

STRENGTH AND GUILE. I couldn't believe what I was seeing. None of us could. This was a member of Special Boat Service. The SBS is to the Royal Marines what the SAS is to the army – its most elite fighting force.

We pinned ourselves to the wall, as if the sheer power of his presence might be enough to knock us all over. We were utterly silent in respect and watched as he stopped to make sure his weapon was clear. When he'd gone, the whispers started. All I could hear was, 'SBS, SBS, did you fucking see fucking SBfuckinS?'

One of the lads said, 'Did you hear about that experiment they did? They took, like, ten Marines who'd only just passed out and put them straight into Special Forces Selection, just to see what would happen.'

'And what happened?' I asked him. 'Don't tell me, they all fucking died.'

'One of them passed,' he said.

'You're shitting me?'

'No, he did,' he said. 'Just one. That's what I heard.'

That morning passed as if in a dream. How did you get to be that SBS guy we'd seen, who had the power to make tough young men fall silent and trained killers cling to the walls? How was it possible? Could *I* do it? If one newly minted Marine had passed Special Forces Selection on one occasion, then why couldn't I?

I completed my Commando course in December 2005 and proposed to Emilie over the Christmas break with a diamond ring from Hatton Garden. When I formally passed out, in January 2006, I was honoured to be awarded the King's Badge award for best recruit, which I'd wear on my left shoulder for the rest of my career. I was posted to Bravo Company, 40 Commando in Taunton, and Emilie and I were moved into married quarters, a smart house two miles from the barracks. We said our vows on 3 May 2006. Sixteen months later I was cutting the umbilical cord of my first daughter, Shyla. I had everything I'd ever wanted: my dagger and my wings, my maroon beret and now my green beret. I also had a beautiful wife and an amazing baby daughter. Then, just ten days after she came into my life, the prediction that nameless Para made in Macedonia when we'd all crowded around that tiny portable television came true. It had all kicked off, and I was posted to Afghanistan.

MY TOUR OF Afghanistan with the Royal Marines was when I realised that the key to leadership lies not just in beating your demons. That's just the start of it. In order to have the edge and strength that a leader needs, you've got to make friends with them too. Lots of people deny their demons. They float through life believing that they're lovely and gentle and wouldn't harm a fly and, when they inevitably do harm that fly, they try to shift responsibility and blame other people. These men and women are not leaders. These are not the people you want guiding you out of that foxhole and through that storm of bullets. If I hadn't understood that, I'd never have made it to the SBS, with whom I served two further tours of Afghanistan.

In the Royal Marines the rules of engagement were strict. We were only allowed to fire our weapons if we were being fired at. This meant that if a man in a field pointed his weapon at us, fired a couple of rounds in our direction, then put his weapon down, we weren't allowed to shoot. If we did, we'd be looking at a court martial and perhaps a prison sentence for murder. It wasn't unusual for men to receive fire from Taliban who'd then simply drop their gun, run to the other side of the field and pick up a rake. There was nothing we could do, and they knew it.

The first time I killed a man it was an ambiguous situation. I'd entered a Taliban compound and a darkened room that was part of it. Out of the shadows came a man in a white dish-dash. He turned towards me and pulled an AK-47 from beneath his clothing. I didn't fire. How did I know he wasn't about to drop it? In that moment I was controlling that demon. But the moment he pointed it towards me, he showed me it was a kill-or-be-killed situation. That's when I accessed my darkness. Two presses on the trigger. Direct hits to the mouth. He was down.

If I hadn't had my demons to call upon I'd probably have hesitated. Was this man a father? Who would he be leaving behind? What devastation would I be inflicting on innocent people? What if I was mistaken? It might have made for a pause of less than a second, but it would have been sufficient to get me killed. And, likewise, if I'd had access to my demons but no control over them, I'd have been spraying bullets everywhere. There are people like that in the services, but I'm not a bully with a weapon. I'm not a person who'll go into a chaotic situation with bad people who I recognise are a threat and kill them automatically. Even in a war zone.

Leaders understand that their demons are an essential part of who they are. By befriending them you're able to call on them when the time comes. Perhaps you're an employer who has had to lay off a lot of staff for the good of the company. Perhaps you need to tell someone who's struggling that they need to try harder. Perhaps you need to tell the person who's leading you some respectful but honest truth. There's no way of doing these things successfully without pushing down on your pedal and letting some darkness come out.

But demons don't become your friends without a fight. And before you take them on, you have to acknowledge that you've got them. From what I've observed, this is one of the reasons servicemen can struggle with Post Traumatic Stress Disorder. For the guys I've spoken with who suffer from PTSD, the problem isn't that they can't process what they've witnessed. It's that they can't process what they've *done*. They've either made a mistake or they've done something that's resulted in carnage. Either that or they can't handle seeing the everyday horrors of war and accept that they're active players in it. If you've synched up with your demons, there's a better chance you'll accept that that's part of you. You're an animal. You have teeth, as very many of earth's creatures do. Once you accept that, it will no longer seem strange that a man who loves his wife and children with all his heart can show up for work one morning and destroy life without thinking.

Making friends with your demons also means accepting that, sometimes, you're a maker of mistakes. Many people I know with PTSD are perfectly able to process the witnessing of death and suffering. What they seem to struggle with more is the fact that they were a cause of it, either as the result of an error or because, in the stress and confusion of the battlefield, they failed to prevent it. Perhaps fear took hold of them, perhaps something within them told them to hide or to shoot recklessly. It seems to me that, because they're in denial of their own potential for causing badness, they play the scene over and over in their heads, working through endless different scenarios: 'What else could I have done to prevent it?'; 'What other decisions could I have made?'; 'Why wasn't it me?' By accessing the darkness that dwells within you, you can accept you made a mistake and move on with your life. You have to be able to not care. If you deny your demons, I'm telling you, they'll take you down.

Now that I'm on civvy street I have to dominate my angry demon. I've been trained to meet violence with extreme violence, but society has zero tolerance for that kind of behaviour. So when I feel the anger rising and I want to strike out, I have to keep it under my command. Control is crucial. Once you've made peace with your dark parts, and have authority over them, you can begin using them to make positives. The same demon that made me violent in the streets of Chelmsford has given me a form of self-defence now. I've lost the fear of being punched or attacked, and this gives me huge power. I also use that violent demon to ramp me up with aggression when I need to get a tough job done. By making friends with your demons, you can take all the darkness that lies within you and create light.

LEADERSHIP LESSONS

Make friends with your demons. Having dark forces living within us is part of being human. They're the result of the inevitable damage of life. Each one of us has a choice: make these demons work for us, or turn them loose against us.

Don't feel bad for going the long way around. When we watch the movies we see people going through hell and coming out the other side a perfect hero. These are fairy tales. In real life we usually have to go through hell and go through hell and go through hell, and only then, if we're lucky, do we learn our lessons – only to half-forget them again. This is nothing to be ashamed of. This is simply the rough and tumble of learning.

Most of us have horror stories we can tell about our childhoods. It's not the horror that defines you, it's how well you've fought it.

Never be afraid to look for help in unlikely places. If I hadn't asked my nan for that address, there's a good chance I'd never have met up with my dad's family. I thought the chances of her helping me were not much better than zero, but you never can tell what's going on in someone else's head. Before dismissing other people, give them a try. You never know who'll turn out to be an unexpected ally.

YOU DON'T NEED TO BE THE LEADER TO LEAD

THE DOOR OF the Chinook began lowering before the helicopter was even on the ground. The stale, still air we'd been breathing for the last hour was instantly dissipated as the outside blasted in. Light flooded over the troop of men sitting in rows, in full kit, their helmets on, their SA80s on their laps. As the helicopter wobbled and bumped to land we moved in single file out into the gale of hot wind and grit that was being thrown up by its enormous blades. The smell was of jet fuel and dried bark. The day was quickly fading, the sun a hazy white button balancing on a distant ridge.

The landscape was barren and strange. It was desert, but not like those glossy images of perfect sand dunes you see in places like the Sahara. This was scrubby and dirty and dotted with tough, thorny-looking shrubs. And it just went on and on, with no particular landmarks other than a bored, ugly river that wound through the scrub. To the north I could see the sombre shadow shapes of a range of low mountains that I'd been informed was infested with Taliban.

It was from there that our base would be regularly attacked with gunfire and RPGs. About a mile to the south was the troubled town of Sangin, in whose streets I'd be operating. Once the Chinook had left us and become just another dot of light in the deep, star-sprayed evening, I was surprised to note that it was also bitterly cold. But I was happy. Here I was. My first war zone.

I'd taken off from RAF Northolt on 21 September 2007 to take part in Operation Herrick 7, which was what they called the British operation in Afghanistan. I'd been made second in command, or 2IC, with direct responsibility for four people in my troop. We'd spent a couple of days acclimatising in the relative comforts of Camp Bastion, a vast base the size of Reading that contained the fifth-busiest UK-operated air strip, not to mention a gym, a Pizza Hut and a non-alcoholic bar called Heroes.

From there we'd been sent to our Forward Operating Base, Sangin District Command or 'Sangin DC', which lay just outside Sangin, a town of 30,000 in Helmand Province. Sangin had a reputation not only as a Taliban town but as a local centre of the heroin trade. With both the Islamists and the drug traffickers violently resisting our presence, it was without doubt the deadliest place in the country at that time. A third of all deaths of British troops during the conflict occurred in Sangin. There was a one in four chance that a man in my position would leave this place injured or killed.

Back at Camp Bastion, dusty and tired returning troops had warned us what to expect. The Taliban would lay IEDs, or 'improvised explosive devices', at night, especially around our base, which had only two entrances and exits. There were two types – contact IEDs, which would explode when stepped on, and command IEDs, which were detonated remotely, usually via Bluetooth. One common tactic the Taliban used involved detonating an IED, then waiting for more troops to arrive and assist the wounded before either detonating another device or attacking with sniper fire.

'You're definitely going to get in a firefight,' one lad told us back at the NAAFI at Bastion. 'People are going to get injured. You should expect a couple of deaths on this tour.'

Hearing this made my blood pump hot. Finally, I'd have the chance to put all my training into practice. As I looked around the table I was surprised to see that some of the other faces didn't seem quite so excited. There was one young man in particular, a nineteen-year-old from Devon called Ian Cressey, who looked like he wanted to run off and ring his mum. I tried to encourage him.

'Sounds fucking hardcore, doesn't it, Cressey?' I said, squeezing his shoulder. I gave him a wink. 'I can't wait. I just want to get in there and kill cunts, yeah?' I joked.

'Same here,' he said.

'Yeah?' I said, squeezing harder now.

'Yes,' he nodded, his eyes wandering to some distant point beyond my left shoulder. 'Kill cunts.'

'That's the spirit, lad.'

I made sure I was sitting next to Cressey in the Chinook out to Sangin DC. I was turning to get a look out of the window when I saw his head was down.

'What's up, dude?' I said, shouting above the colossal racket of the helicopter.

'I'm good,' he said, with a thin smile. 'Can't wait. Kill cunts, mate.'

'You can talk to me,' I said. 'You know that, don't you? Whenever you need to, just grab me.'

'No, I'm good,' he said. 'Cheers, Ant. I'm fine.'

But within thirty seconds, he was examining his thumbs again, his face the colour of yesterday's porridge.

This was a worry. It wasn't only that Cressey was one of the four men I'd have immediate responsibility for in Sangin. We were going into a war zone, and in that environment it would only take one man with his mind tuned out to fuck the whole thing up. I knew that I'd die for my men, every single one of them. I needed to be sure that every single one of them would die for me. That was the only way we'd all make it out of Sangin with our hearts still beating and the blood it was pumping finding four limbs. But the way it was looking right now, the only thing Cressey was dying for was a ticket back to London Heathrow. I'd made Emilie a solemn promise that I'd come home alive. When I'd made that promise I had no doubt I could keep to it. But what I didn't need were weaknesses in my troop. And Cressey was beginning to look like one.

Forty minutes into the flight, as we neared Sangin DC, we began to draw machine-gun fire. The helicopter banked suddenly and swerved, the windows opposite us emptying of sky and showing only the sand and rocks of the plains of Helmand far below. I winked at Cressey excitedly. Before long we righted ourselves and were landing.

The base was an old bombed-out Afghan compound that had been commandeered by our military. There was nothing pretty or comfortable about it. Half the walls were pimpled with bullet holes and shrapnel spray from bomb blasts, the other half weren't there anymore and were now just sandbags. Us troops would live and sleep in mud huts and socialise around a simple fire pit. Other more permanent but still heavily war-damaged buildings housed the offices of our people, along with some local-government personnel and members of the Afghan police.

I, and many of the other lads, were wary of these guys. The previous year the Taliban had retaken Sangin town, and Sangin DC had spent several months in a state of siege, suffering fierce attacks almost every day. Afterwards it was discovered that the Afghan police had been leaking information to the Taliban about its layout and operation. The siege had ended five months earlier, having lasted from June 2006 to April 2007. It had taken two hundred paratroopers, with the help of seven hundred men from various allied forces, to finally break it. These Talibs weren't fucking about.

But even with the base free, the Taliban wasn't prepared to let the town go without a serious battle. The fighting continued until April 2007, when a thousand coalition troops finally recaptured it as part of Operation Silver. And now that we had it back, we had to keep it. This was where me and my boys came in. 40 Commando had to maintain a show of strength, which meant fourteen-hour foot patrols up and down the war-damaged streets, fully armed and laden with kit. We'd go out in three teams of eight, one upfront, one in the middle and one behind. We wanted the locals to look at us and think, 'Fucking hell, they're a force to be reckoned with.' But it wasn't just a case of wartime policing and the display of power. We had to maintain a balance. On our patrols we'd try to help the locals out where we could, often with medical attention, while gathering as much intelligence from them as was possible.

Hearts and minds were crucial, but in reality the job mostly involved getting from A to B to C to D. The town itself was largely abandoned, the shutters closed on all the businesses apart from a couple of shops selling the usual essentials: SIM cards from the local networks – Roshan, MTN, Afghan Telecom – blue tins of chicken sausages, packets of Pine and Wave cigarettes, shit crisps, scratched glass bottles of Coca-Cola in knackered fridges, the logo in Arabic script, and slightly squashed cartons of mango and pineapple juice. We'd usually only spot the occasional person running here and there. When the locals saw our troop approaching they'd go into lockdown, hiding in their compounds.

Our patrols were tough, physically and mentally. We'd be in full body armour, with front and back plates and side protection, and I had an additional cop vest for good measure. As well as all this, we'd have twelve full magazines apiece, each containing thirty rounds, together with four grenades and six litres of water to last us the day. We'd stop for lunch and eat rations – bacon and beans, corned-beef hash or beef stew – but I'd make my lads have them cold. I didn't want to waste time heating food up, and the last thing I needed was them staggering around feeling lethargic. We'd usually have a brew going, so at least there'd be something hot in their stomachs. The whole break would be over in ten minutes. We'd always make sure our movements were as unpredictable as possible. The Taliban could never hope to take us on toe-to-toe, so instead would play a sneaky-beaky game. If they were able to predict where we'd be at a certain time, they'd be able to strike, either with IEDs, suicide idiots or sniper fire from high buildings.

Just two days after our arrival we got the news that our troop sergeant had to return to the UK because his wife had fallen from a horse and broken her back. In the shuffle upwards, I went from section 2IC to section commander, an unusual promotion for someone with my experience. Now I had responsibility for eight men, and had to carry a pistol and extra ammunition in my day sack, which weighed between fifty and sixty pounds.

As the days ground on I was growing increasingly worried about some of the lads, not least Cressey. On some mornings I'd seen him actually vomit with fear as he was preparing to leave the base and, right now, he was staring at the dirt, sighing and grumbling about his cold beans.

'Get your fucking head up,' I said to him. 'You're a Royal Marine in a fucking war zone. Suck it up.'

'I'm trying, Ant.'

'Trying's not fucking good enough.'

I hoped I was getting the balance right, but it was tricky. I had to keep Cressey sharp, yet at the same time I was worried that if I just drilled him further into the ground he'd become even more of a liability. While it was my job to keep him motivated, I also believed that the Royal Marines should consist of positive, self-motivated people.

When I wasn't sure how to act and was tempted to give Cressey or one of the others a heavy blast I'd sometimes ask myself, 'What would Dad have done?' I'd often give them the sharp end when they needed it and then later on, maybe at night around the fire, I'd have a more gentle talk in private. It was usually pretty effective with most of them, but nothing seemed to be working with Cressey. I could see it in his face – he was counting down the days and the hours. He wasn't organised with his kit, either. I was always careful to take all the rounds out of the magazine of my weapon, because if you don't it weakens the spring. Worse-case scenario: you could fire half your magazine, only for it to fail. To avoid this, I'd ease my spring every now and then and oil it up. I'd shown Cressey this more than once and impressed upon him what might happen if his weapon jammed during a firefight. But he'd made it very clear he couldn't give a fuck.

It all came to a head one night when we received letters from home. Letters had always been a bit of a sore point for me. Before going to war it was mandated that every man had to write a letter for their family to receive in the event of their death. I'd refused point-blank but, after my arrival at Sangin DC, my sergeant major had pulled me up about it.

'You're not getting out of this, Middleton,' he told me. 'Write anything you want. Just get it done.'

'OK, Sergeant Major,' I said.

I took the sheet of paper he'd handed me back to my quarters and wrote 'The good die young, and I don't want to disappoint anyone' on it, before slotting it neatly back into its envelope. That evening, my sergeant major came to find me, my envelope in his hand.

'Middleton, you fucking lunatic. I can't fucking send this to your wife.'

'I don't want to put anything,' I said.

'Why not? What about your family? What about your daughter?'

'What about them? I'm not going to die. Simple as.'

He walked off, laughing, and shaking his head.

Unlike the rest of the lads, I'd decided never to call home. I'd also given Emilie strict instructions not to write to me. I just didn't want to know what was happening back there. Any domestic problems my wife or children might be going through would only distract me, just as reminding myself how much I missed Emilie would make me lose focus. I know this sounds harsh. But the fact is that when you're in the field you can't afford a second's hesitation. You can't allow a single drip of negativity or worry to get in. You need to be able to dodge bullets out there. Your awareness has to be keen enough that you can anticipate exactly what's going to happen next. You just can't do that if you're thinking about the broken dishwasher or the rash on your kid's arse. It was much more important that I came back alive.

This was why I was surprised and nervous when the mail was handed out as we were sitting around the campfire and I was handed an envelope with Emilie's handwriting on it. Had something happened back home? Something serious enough to force Emilie to contact me? I was staring at the letter, the fire hot on my face, not knowing what to do with it, when I noticed Cressey beside me, frantically opening his latest note from home. Then he stood up and walked away.

I gave him a few seconds and then followed him discreetly. I found him on his knees behind one of the mud huts, sobbing, strings of phlegm in the corners of his lips.

'It's Hannah,' he said. 'I knew it. She's been shagging my fucking c-cousin.'

I crouched down so I was on his level.

'Listen, fuck her,' I said. 'Fuck Hannah. She's clearly not worth your time.'

He nodded his head.

'You've got to straighten yourself up. I need to know you're not going to let this take you down. I know I've been on your back a bit since we got here, but it's for a reason. I'm trying to keep us all alive. I'm trying to keep you alive. That's the most important thing to me. Making sure you get out of here in one piece.'

I put my hands on his shoulders. 'I'm not bullshitting you. Look at me.'

He raised his chin and met my eye.

'I would take a bullet for you. I would die for you, without hesitation. Do you understand?'

His breathing slowed. His sobs quietened.

'What I need is for you to be in the frame of mind where you'd take a bullet for me.'

He nodded. 'Thanks, Ant.'

'Don't thank me. Go to your bed, have a good cry, punch some walls, and I'll see you tomorrow, a new man. Yes?'

'Yes, Ant,' he said.

I watched him pace towards his hut. Then I went back to the others, took Emilie's letter out of my shirt pocket and threw it into the fire.

*   *   *

ANOTHER WEEK, ANOTHER challenge. A new troop sergeant had arrived in Sangin DC to replace the one who'd returned to the UK to tend to his injured wife. This meant I had to step back down to my 2IC role. In the days before he came, rumours began swirling around the Forward Operational Base (FOB). Our new boss was a guy called Lionel Boyle. He was known as a 'Lympstonite' because he'd spent years – pretty much his entire career – back at Lympstone Commando, training recruits. He'd never seen action, never been on ops. 'And he talks to the lads like shit,' said one man, who knew him from the training centre. 'He's dick-meat. Pure cock.' But I decided not to listen to the gossip. I'd form my own opinion of the man.

On the morning of his arrival, I handed in the pistol that had been granted to me as troop sergeant and waited to meet him. A couple of hours later I was chatting with a buddy outside my mud hut when I saw a man who could only have been Boyle coming briskly towards me from the direction of the officers' block. You could always tell the new arrivals: they were so scrubbed and fresh and clean-shaven, with the sun shining in the tips of their boots.

I held out my hand. 'I'm Ant,' I said. 'I was section commander, but since you came back I'm now 2IC again.'

'OK,' he said, shaking it lightly. 'And what's been happening out there?'

'We're covering a lot of ground, things are going pretty steadily. It's fine. No complaints. And, just to let you know,

I've handed my pistol in, so we're all good to go tomorrow.'

'And your pistol was signed over by a qualified operative, I take it?'

'Qualified?' I said. 'Well, I handed it over to the section commander.'

He looked at me with paternal exasperation, as if he'd found exactly the shambles he'd been fearing. He was livid about it.

'Dear God,' he said. 'You have to go through the proper procedure. You can't just fling your weapon over and say "Here's your pistol." It has to be done properly, in the presence of a recognised witness, and given to someone qualified to take it in. The serial number needs to be recorded, the paperwork signed. Did you follow this procedure, Middleton?'

'Well, I ...'

'I said, did you follow this procedure?'

'No, Sergeant.'

'For fuck's sake, this is a war zone, Middleton,' he snapped, working himself up into a headmasterly rage. He took a small step back. 'And you've been acting section commander?'

There was a silence.

'Right, get all the lads and line them up.'

A war zone? What did he know about a war zone? For a start, in a war zone you don't line up on parade as you would back at base. It's different out in the field. It's not all boot-shined and spit-polished. You loosen things up a bit – you shave every other day, not every day, and you let your sideburns grow. It's a morale thing, a bit of leeway to see you through the shit. I couldn't believe what I was hearing.

'You want us all lined up?' I said. 'Out there? All the lads?'

'Five minutes.'

Five minutes later there we were, all present and correct outside our huts, feeling like a bunch of knobs. Boyle was marching up and down in front of us with his hands behind his back like he was in his Lympstone parade square.

'Look at the state of you,' he said. 'You're a fucking disgrace. How have you let yourselves slide like this? You're Royal Marines. There are standards, gentlemen, and being on the battlefield does not excuse you from them. I want you back here in ten minutes with your sideburns shaved to the middle of your ears.'

We filed away and got in a huddle behind one of the huts.

'How are we going to deal with this bloke?' said someone.

Nobody answered.

'Let me deal with it,' I said. 'I'll sort him out.'

Some of the lads wanted to fight back, but I knew that would have been a bad idea. Although the Chelmsford street-fighter in me would have found great satisfaction in putting a crack right down the centre of Boyle's jawbone, I'd come a long way from there. Those demons were now working for me. I knew the aggressive approach would very quickly have left us with no power at all. We'd only push him into coming back at us even harder. The more we went in on him, the more he'd have to elevate himself over us in order to keep hold of his self-respect. In a matter of days we'd have created a monster.

Those next few weeks were a master's degree in wily leadership. The most crucial lesson I learned was that, to be a successful leader, you have to be emotionally connected. This is especially true when you're not officially in a position of authority and have to manipulate someone above you in the pecking order. To do this, you've got to pick up on all their wants and needs and insecurities. You work out how they see the world and let that guide you.

To me it was obvious that Boyle was a stickler for detail and used arbitrary signs, like the length of our sideburns, as a yardstick to judge how well things were going. But I also knew it went much deeper than that. What Boyle really wanted, deep down in his delicate little pigeon heart, was the respect of the lads. He wanted us to look up to him. He wanted that with all his soul and body. He'd reacted so unreasonably and disproportionately about the length of our sideburns because he'd taken it as a sign of personal rejection. It was as if we'd collectively blown raspberries at him in the school playground. This, I realised, was my way in.

As soon as I worked out what was really going on, I started to feel quite sorry for him. But I also knew I couldn't have him treating the lads like that. So, over the next few days I started making an effort to befriend him. I didn't particularly want to spend my downtime hanging out with Lionel Boyle, drinking coffee with him and flattering his ego, but I had to remember my objective. It isn't sitting in a certain office or having a certain job title or a badge on your chest that makes you a leader. Sometimes it's simply putting the group first in order to get the job done. And that's what I was doing.

Meanwhile, I told the lads to keep their facial hair in order, at least for now. There were a few grumbles about this – and I didn't blame them. The last thing we wanted to be worried about when we got up in the morning was having a shave. We wanted to be preparing our kit, getting ready for a long day walking those sweating, deadly streets, feeling constantly surrounded by eyes and sudden noises and shadows behind doors. But I knew, if we were to ever get him off our backs, we'd have to give him this little sign.

On the evenings after long patrols I started spending more and more time chatting with him, sympathising with him, making him mugs of coffee. 'Are you alright, Sergeant? What's been happening?' I'd overplay it. It was toy respect. But it was my opportunity to make him think I was letting him into the fold, which was where I was convinced he really wanted to be, even if he himself didn't consciously know it.

Before long he'd learned to trust me. That's when I felt able to subtly start changing the way he recognised respect and success, slowly turning his head in a new direction, shifting his focus. I'd emphasise how hard the guys had worked and how completely devoted they were to their mission.

'Cor, that was a long patrol,' I'd say. 'The lads have come in and they've cleaned their weapons and they're now getting their heads down because they're up early in the morning on another one. I'll make sure they're up at first light and we're ready to go.' Rather than, 'They're thinking about shaving,' I'd make it, 'They're thinking about the job at hand.'

Boyle had his Lympstonite book that he was devoted to. What I was doing was adding extra pages to it. And it worked. Within a fortnight our sideburns were creeping down our faces, and he was happy and leaving us be. Life was returning to normal.

WE WERE OUT on patrol when we just happened to be in the vicinity of our base at somewhere around lunchtime.

'All right, lads. Special treat,' I said. 'Let's hop back into the fob and have a cooked meal.'

We settled down in the relative safety of Sangin DC and lit our burners, happily anticipating beans, stew and corned beef hash served hot, for once, just as God intended. The bubbles had just started popping on the surface of my bacon and beans when I became aware of a commotion over by one of the offices. It was Boyle. Now he was running towards us, his face long and pale, his eyes bright.

'Quick!' he shouted. 'Get your kit back on!'

I stood up. 'What's happening, Sergeant?'

'An IED,' he said, between puffs of breath. 'Two kilometres to the west. We've taken injuries, maybe worse. We need to get out there now as a QRF.'

Minutes later, Boyle and the rest of us were marching out of the front entrance of Sangin DC as a Quick Response Force, helmets and headsets on, SA80s ready, all thoughts of lunch a long-forgotten dream. The forty minutes it took us to reach the IED site passed as if in seconds. All twenty-four of us fell into that strange, zoomed-in state in which nothing else exists but the mission. The heat, the fear, the aches, the pains, the sweat, the sores, the thoughts of family and home, the human politics of Boyle, Cressey and all the rest of it had gone completely. The entire universe vanished around us and the only thing that was left was one foot in front of the other.

The incident had taken place outside a typical Afghan compound. It was a large, two-storey structure built from dried, compacted mud, which took up the area of roughly half a football pitch. Inside the compound would be a maze of darkened rooms that could either have been booby-trapped or have Taliban fighters lurking in its shadows, armed with grenades and AK-47s or strapped up in suicide vests. You couldn't have imagined a more unpredictable environment if you were a designer of first-person shooter video games. The level of adrenalised fearfulness inside that dusty shithole would be high.

We gathered around Boyle, awaiting further information that he'd been receiving on his radio.

'All right lads, huddle in,' he said. 'An officer has been blown up. We're going to clear the area, then retrieve his remains so they can be sent home. The IED went off over by the south wall of the compound. That's where his arms and legs are. His torso is on the roof.' He turned to me. 'Middleton.'

'Yes, Sergeant?'

'Take one of the lads, clear the compound and retrieve the torso.'

I glanced around at the other lads, looking for a suitable candidate. Immediately this tough-nut Welshman called Miles stepped forward. Ordinarily he'd have been my automatic choice, and he knew it. But to his surprise and mine I found myself nodding past him to a familiar face hiding at the back of the huddle.

'Cressey,' I said. 'Come on, mate. Come with me.'

Miles was respectful enough not to say anything, but I could tell by his face that he thought I'd fucking lost it.

I walked around the corner with Cressey to the door of the compound. 'What I'm going to do is put a grenade in each room,' I told him.

'A grenade?'

'That's how we'll clear the building. You've got to cover me as I go in. OK?'

'OK,' he said.

'It'd better be, mate,' I said. 'We don't know what kind of badness is in there. I'm relying on you, one hundred per cent.'

'I've got it,' he said. 'I'm good.'

We stacked up against the door, which wasn't bolted and hung slightly ajar. I kicked it open, unpinned a grenade and tossed it in. For the crucial moments between my appearance in the doorway and the blast, I had only Cressey to protect me. They were very long moments. And then, boom! Out of the building came a barrage of grit, sound and wind. The instant it settled we moved into the space, exactly as we'd been trained, each covering a different corner. Then we stacked up against the next door. And that's how we did it, the entire building.

Before long we located the entrance to the roof. We crept up the short flight of steps and pushed at the door, which opened with a rusty groan. For a moment it was if all that existed on the other side was a realm of pure, blinding light. Our vision quickly adjusting, we stepped out into the heat that beat hard on the back of our necks.

It was about six feet in front of us, not far from the edge. It was fully clothed and, because its owner had perished in a blast, the heart had stopped pumping instantly, so there was no blood. It didn't look human. It looked like a thing – a package ready for posting or a piece of a resuscitation doll. Under the torn shirt you could just make out a ragged disc of meat from where, just this morning, an arm had brushed teeth and made coffee.

'You all right?' I said to Cressey.

'Yes, Ant.'

He meant it too. I glanced over my shoulder to see his gaze fixed on the body part. There was a fire in his eyes I'd never seen before.

'Fucking cowards,' he muttered.

'Give me a hand,' I said.

We grabbed a shoulder each and dragged it across the roof, then carefully lowered it down, into the waiting hands of the men on the ground, where the torso was placed on a stretcher next to its arms and legs. Cressey was all business.

'Good man,' I said to him, as we moved back into the compound.

'I just want to …'

'Kill cunts?'

He nodded grimly. 'Fucking *kill* cunts.'

We arrived back at base fired up and mostly silent, each man in their own space of shock and fury. Just then, as we were clearing our weapons, there was the unmistakable ricocheting crack of a round being fired. It came from inside the compound. Everyone flinched and went to ground, grabbing for their weapons. Everyone, that is, except for one man. Over in the corner, looking red-faced and sheepish, was Cressey. He'd made a basic error, a 'negligent discharge'. He must have cocked his weapon before taking the magazine off, rather than taking the magazine off first to extract the round. But there was no harm done: he'd done everything else correctly, and the round had just fired harmlessly into the dirt.

As the lads slowly and wearily rose to their feet, Boyle stormed furiously towards us.

'You! Cressey!' he said. 'You fucking idiot. I'm sending you back to Camp Bastion. You're getting charged.'

I couldn't believe what I was hearing. I'd never wanted so badly to knock someone out.

'Sergeant,' I said, blocking his path towards him. 'Come on.'

But he ignored me. When he was done with Cressey I followed him back to his office and closed the door behind me.

'This isn't right,' I said. 'It's going to be a serious mark on his record. He's a young lad. He's just turned a corner. If you charge him, everyone's going to know about it. This is going to knock his fucking confidence badly.'

He sat himself down behind his desk, then said with a contemptuous sneer, 'And they gave *you* the King's Badge?'

Savage electricity charged through the fingers of my right

hand, trying to curl them into a fist. But I wouldn't let him have it. I was my father's son, not my stepfather's.

I went back to my mud hut fuming. Leadership isn't about throwing the book at someone the moment they fuck up. It's not about saying, 'I've made my way through the ranks and this is what the book says, so follow it or suffer.' That book is not followed by leaders, it's written by them. We were a team operating in a risky situation. What message does that send? What's going to happen when things go wrong, as they inevitably will, out there on the battlefield? The very reason you can operate outside of your comfort zone in a dangerous situation is that you know the people behind you and above you will be there when you fall. If Cressey made the same mistake again, fair enough. But I could guarantee he wouldn't.

I soon decided that my game of manipulation with Boyle had reached its limit. I walked over to the office of my sergeant major.

'Come in,' he said.

It was dark outside and the only light came from a single low-wattage bulb hanging off a wire. There were maps on the wall, mosquitos in the air, and the smell and crackle of the fire getting going outside. The sergeant major sat behind his desk, the dim yellow light casting shadows off the lines in his face.

'What can I do for you, Ant?' he asked.

'It's Boyle. I need to talk to you about him, sir,' I said.

'Go on.'

'He wants to send Cressey back for a court martial. I don't think it's the right thing to do. He was up there with me on the roof today, recovering body parts, and he didn't fucking flinch. And it's not as if he's shot anyone. He had his weapon pointed into the sand. No harm done, you know? He's not the most confident of lads as it is. I've been working really hard with him, building him up, and I was getting somewhere. Today was a breakthrough. I saw it in him, that strength coming out. Sending him to Bastion will destroy him.'

He put his glasses on the desk and leaned back in his chair.

'You're asking me to overrule Boyle?'

I shrugged. 'To be honest, all the lads are out of joint with him a bit. He's been poking people, coming in with all his drill stuff. He doesn't get it.'

He sighed deeply.

I said, 'I guarantee you, personally, that Cressey will not do that again. Ever.'

In the end I got my way. Cressey wasn't sent back for a court martial. And from that point on, everything Boyle said to any of us was just white noise. It wasn't long before he was spending the majority of his time hiding in the ops room away from the rest of us. Even though I wasn't the official leader, in practice I was back in charge.

That night, after I left the sergeant major's office, I did what I always did on returning from a long day in the field.

I went to the bombed-out top floor of the building at the centre of the base, jumped on the rusty, squeaky bicycle that had been put on a stand, and began working out under a huge full moon that illuminated the outline of the dark, dangerous mountains as brightly as if it were God's own torch. I couldn't help but feel disillusioned with my first experience of war. I'd come to Afghanistan full of excitement for the challenge but felt limited by our timid rules of engagement, and that I was endangered by people who just didn't give a shit and shouldn't have been there. In a matter of days, though, none of this would matter any longer.

Ever since that fateful day during Commando training when I'd seen that man leaving the armoury wearing a green beret with the motto BY STRENGTH AND GUILE, I'd wanted one thing above all else. To join the Special Boat Service. I'd heard a rumour that there'd once been a Marine who was fresh from passing out who'd made it into the Special Forces. I had no idea if it was really true, but the truth of it no longer mattered. I would make it true. I would achieve what that possibly mythical lad had. Back in May my sergeant major had signed me off as a candidate. The forms had been sent. I'd been excited about it ever since. And now, finally, the time had come. I was leaving my tour three months early. I was going home. I'd spend three precious hours with my family, and then, at 6 a.m., I was off to Wales, where I'd start my Special Forces Selection.

LEADERSHIP LESSONS

You don't need to be a leader to lead. Very often in life you'll find yourself in a situation in which the person officially in charge is not doing the greatest job. If you decide to take matters into your own hands, you need to do it cleverly. A certain skill for manipulation is often what's called for. You need to get under that leader's skin, win their trust and discover what they want. As long as they think they're getting it, you're free to steer the ship.

Never be too quick to write anyone off. Even though I sensed Ian Cressey would be able to handle the recovery of that body, the level of professionalism he brought to the situation still surprised me. Since then, I've always been extremely careful about being too hasty with my judgements of those who appear weak. There's often steel inside them – they just need the opportunity to show it.

Do what you have to, even if people judge you for it. I know some of the lads probably found my attitude to letters and calls to my family harsh or unfeeling. But I had my reasons, and I wasn't going to let their preconceptions bully me into not doing what I knew was best for me.

FAILURE ISN'T MAKING THE MISTAKE, IT'S ALLOWING THE MISTAKE TO WIN

THE INSTRUCTIONS WERE simple: be in the galley at Sennybridge Military Training Area in South Wales at 9 a.m. on 5 January 2008. I arrived fifteen minutes early and found myself a seat right at the front, tucked into a far corner, and watched the room slowly fill up with chattering men. Soon, every seat was taken. By the top of the hour they were lining the walls, more than two hundred of them, each individual with the fitness of a professional athlete. These were the best: the hardest, fiercest, strongest, brightest, most relentless and wily soldiers that the combined British armed forces could produce.

We were Intake 0801; 08 for the year, and 01 because we were the first course of the two that would take place annually. Selection was a six-month ordeal, and this first 'hill phase' would comprise four weeks in the Brecon Beacons. As the January group, we had to endure 'Winter Hills', which is a lot tougher than 'Summer Hills,' the seasonal Welsh weather being a bitter and remorseless enemy.

Bang on time a side door opened up. The chatter turned instantly to near-silence, the only remaining sound being a few people going, 'Sssshhh, sssshhh.' The man who entered was in his forties, bald and decked out in tan-patterned jungle kit. Around his waist was a blue SAS belt. There was something about this individual that simply commanded respect. You couldn't fake the sense of ability and experience that came off him. It was as if everything he'd witnessed and pushed himself through had become part of his sinew and bones. He was a living, breathing, walking, talking lump of human power and his presence entered the room like an avalanche. He strode up to the lectern and smacked his folder down onto it, the slap echoing loudly around the walls.

'Right,' he said. 'Listen in everyone. I'm your chief instructor. You will address me as "Staff" at all times. If I ever see you in front of me, it'll either be because you've fucked up badly and I'm about to fuck you off, or you're injured and I'm sorting your ticket home. It's very simple. You don't want to be up in front of me. And neither do you want to be pestering me or any of the directing staff. Everything you need to know will be posted on that noticeboard over there by the door every night – times, locations, kit lists, everything. Read it. Do what it says. That's it.'

His eyes slowly swept the crowd.

'Gentlemen, I don't give a fuck who you are or where you've come from. You're all at the same level now. You need to get it into your heads that most of you will fail this course.'

He pointed to a table right over the sea of heads at the far corner of the room. It had perhaps eight or nine people sitting round it.

'In six months' time, that's the number of men who'll still be with us.'

I craned my neck to see the table. It seemed a very, very long way away.

With that, eight instructors emerged from the side door and stood in formation behind the chief instructor and stared straight through us, as if into an empty room. The place was now eerily quiet. There was no coughing or throat clearing, no rustling of clothing. To even be acknowledged by these men, you'd have to get through the toughest military course on the planet. We were guests visiting in their world, probably briefly, and they were letting us know it.

Some of the guys around me paled. You could see the doubts crowding in on them. They were either thinking they weren't good enough or were simply scared shitless. You could hardly blame them – after all, it's not uncommon for people to die on selection. One guy had recently passed away due to heat exhaustion, another was running from a hunter force, during the escape and evasion section, and went over a cliff. Both incidents had caused headlines and handwringing in the papers but, if you ask me, that's just the kind of thing that happens when you're trying to weed the strongest from the not-quite-strong-enough. It irritated me when I heard people blame the army for these deaths. If I died, I'd want people to know it was because I wanted it so badly that I'd pushed myself so much and paid the ultimate price. I'd want people to be proud of me, not making excuses.

But still, the fact that these deaths had happened at all brought it home to me. When I'd started other military courses, I'd looked at those who'd already passed and thought, 'That's going to be me.' Now I caught myself thinking, 'I *want* that to be me.' This was different. It was a new feeling and, in that moment in the galley, I'll honestly admit I felt overwhelmed. Nothing could've been more important for me than passing Selection. I couldn't go back to the Royal Marines after my depressing experience trudging the streets of Sangin.

I'd already decided. If I didn't make it into the Special Forces, then that would be it. I'd leave the military. I knew that the failure would shatter my sense of who I was and what my life was all about. The goal of passing Selection was all that was keeping me together. The blood, anger and confusion of life outside the Forces had been soothed by having this distant point of light to focus on. I knew this was going to be the hardest challenge I'd ever have to endure, but I'd give everything I had to make it. I'd give my life.

*   *   *

I'D ARRIVED AT Sennybridge two hours earlier, the suspension of my Silver Renault Clio suffering under the weight of all my kit. I knew I was getting close to the base when I began recognising the names of local pubs that were familiar to me from all the myths and legends about Selection I'd heard down the years – there was The Red Lion, there was The Tanner's Arms. As I drove further into the area along a narrow country road, the hills only seemed to grow higher and crueller. Most people, driving this route, would probably be marvelling at the natural beauty, but the more magnificent the scenery became, the more intimidated I felt. All I could think was, 'I'm going to be pounding over that fucking thing with a big fucking bergen on my back.' I could feel all the old insecurities about running with weight rushing back into me. Yes, I'd managed to pull myself up Craphat Hill – after a struggle – but Craphat Hill was a hump in the road compared with what was about to happen here.

After parking up, I dropped my kit off at the student accommodation, which was a basic wooden hut lined with bunks for forty or so men, one of six that housed us all. I walked in to see a handful of guys gathered in the centre of the room. They were doing that getting-to-know-you thing, chatting too fast, laughing too loudly, eyeballing each other, measuring up the competition. The mindset among many of them seemed to be that this would be a contest, that we would be battling each other out there. I knew the smartest approach would be to keep the competition internal; make the battle solely with myself.

It didn't look like anyone had established a bed yet, so I kept my eyes down, shuffled past them and headed straight to a bunk in the far corner, where I began unpacking, hanging up my kit, placing my socks and boots in such a way that I could easily and swiftly grab them.

On the drive up I'd consciously decided not to get into the whole 'I'm here to make friends' routine. I knew the best strategy was to avoid the loud lads, especially the ones who'd been on Selection before and were giving it the gobshite treatment, and those who'd never done it but were Selection nerds and having a whale of a time broadcasting all the dubious information they'd found on internet forums and in squaddy pubs. These were the men who were going to highlight themselves to the DSs and I didn't want to be anywhere near them. My plan was to deliberately isolate myself, to be the grey man: quiet, unnoticed, focused only on what was important – passing Selection.

When the briefing with the chief instructor was over, the men of intake 08:01 filed out of the galley, subdued and thoughtful. I hung back, peeled off and made a diversion to the washrooms, where I waited for a while in the hope of avoiding once more the getting-to-know-you traps. It was a good move. When I got back to the accommodation block they were all at it again, bunched up and in groups. Aside from me, nobody had even claimed a bed yet, let alone started squaring their kit away.

Nobody, that is, except one man. I could see him as I neared the end of the block. I couldn't believe it. Out of all thirty-nine of the free bunks, he'd chosen the one right next to me. This was fucking perfect. The last thing I wanted was some idiot who was searching for a best buddy. As I approached I tried to rapidly get the measure of him. He was standing up, seeing to his kit, and was about the same height and build as me, but holy shit, he was one of the ugliest men I'd ever seen in my life. I could see from his uniform that he was a Royal Engineer. I'd have to keep my own Engineer past quiet – the last thing I needed was a bonding session with some great, gobby, piss-drinking wanker.

I sat down on my bed and he turned to me, a typical hard man. Give him a club, put him in a leopard-skin nappy, make him smash rocks all day and he'd be happy.

'Mate, I hope you don't mind if I jump in,' he said earnestly, his eyes wide.

I knew instantly that I'd got this guy wrong. He wasn't searching for a pal. He'd had exactly the same idea as me. He was tucking himself away. Smart lad.

'No, don't be silly,' I said warmly. 'You crack on.'

'I'm Darren, by the way,' he said.

'Anthony.'

'Different world, eh?' he said, as he turned back to his unpacking.

'Seems it.'

Although we weren't about to have a merry chat about it, I knew exactly what Darren meant. The differences between the SBS and SAS and the rest of the armed forces run deep. With the Special Forces, you're taking all the alpha males out of all the tribes of the military and putting them together in one elite group. There were no sheep here, only shepherds. They're not Yes men of the kind that the Lympstonite Boyle loved. They possess both physical and intellectual stamina, and have to be able to use initiative and strategy under the toughest of circumstances – whether they're starving, exhausted, trapped, injured, lost, being tortured or having a gun pointed at their skull by a screaming Talib – or all of these put together. This culture begins at Selection. No one's chasing you up to do anything. You're simply told where to be, at what time and with what kit. If you're late, you get a black tick. Two black ticks and you're gone. That was it. No sympathy, no excuses, no second chances. And that's exactly the way it should be.

While the other lads continued their dick-measuring, I went to bed early, my bladder freshly full. One good thing about those long patrols in Sangin had been the opportunity they'd given me for tactical planning. I'd come up with a special routine that I promised myself I'd stick to every night on Selection. Before going to sleep I'd drink a litre of water from a bottle I'd stash beside my bed. About three hours later, I'd be awake, in desperate need of a piss. I knew the washrooms were bound to be in a separate building. That meant I'd have to leave the accommodation block in my boxers and flip-flops in the freezing, wet winter weather. I'd get up, go out, take a piss, fill my bottle again and neck it as I walked back to the block. My goal was to be always pissing clear. That would mean I was fully hydrated. We'd be marching with loaded bergens, but the weight they stipulated for each march wouldn't include food and water. My routine meant I'd be able to go out with less liquid, which meant gaining a small but perhaps decisive advantage.

6 A.M. A freezing parade square, the air shredded by horizontal rain. More than two hundred hunched silhouettes, men sitting on bergens in the darkness. The harsh white beams of four tonners were shining over them, their engines growling. It hadn't even begun and already the grimness of Selection laid heavy.

Picked out in the lights of the truck was the chief instructor.

'Numbers one to fifty on wagon one. Fifty-one to 101 on wagon two ...'

When it was my turn I hauled myself into the back and put another plan into action. These four tonners that were used throughout the military for moving troops had long benches running up the middle and sides on which the men would sit facing outwards. As my group settled in, I zipped right underneath the centre bench. I unrolled my sleeping bag, laid it over myself and closed my eyes. The seating above my head filled up and I could hear the Selection nerds giving out: 'Right, I know where we're fucking going. It's fucking Elan, and you follow this goat path …'

I've always had the ability to drop off to sleep whenever I wanted and, lulled by the rumble of the engine, I was soon catching up on some of the shuteye I'd missed the night before. Forty-five minutes later, the noise ceased. Within seconds, my sleeping bag was back in my bergen, and I was on my feet and out. We were in a gravel car park surrounded by hills that were steep, covered in shale and scrub, wreathed in cloud and wet.

'OK, all right, this is a Combat Fitness Test, yes?' barked one of the DS. 'Every ten minutes a member of the directing staff will take another thirty men. The course is eight miles. You have two hours.'

When it was my turn to launch off, I quickly found myself in the front, fifty-five-pound bergen on, my weapon in my hands. It felt good to be leading. But it was a mistake. I slowed down, letting the panting bodies overtake me, until I was comfortably in the middle. There was no way I was going to highlight myself, and I also knew how my mind worked. If I came first, I'd only start putting pressure on myself to start coming first in everything. The last man I needed as an enemy in all this was myself. So that's how I played it for the rest of the day, through all the physical trials. That evening, following an advanced map-reading test, I walked back into the accommodation and noticed that four beds were now empty. It had begun.

And that's how it continued, day after day. The goal of the directing staff was not to help us through the course, it was to help us out of the door. They wanted to thin out the crowd. For them, every walker was another victory. A man could be taken off Selection at any time on any day of any week. I'd heard that some got through every phase of the course, or even the entire six months of Selection, only to be told they hadn't passed right at the end because they didn't fit the mould.

It was more common, though, for a man to hand in their 'VW', which stands for 'Voluntary Withdrawal'. One guy I could tell wasn't going to quit in a hurry was the one in the bed next to me. Unexpectedly, Darren and I quickly grew close. On the second day he passed me coming back from the showers with a towel round my waist and spotted my tattoo.

'Fuckin' hell, were you an Engineer?' he asked.

'Oh,' I said, glancing at my tattoo with fake surprise, as if I'd completely forgotten it was there. 'Oh yeah, that's right.'

'But you're wearing a Royal Marine beret?'

'Yes, mate,' I said. 'I used to be in 9 Parachute Squadron.'

'Well, holy shit, lad,' he said, his face breaking out into an astonished grin.

And that was it. Before long, Darren and I were inseparable. We'd sit together, eat together, do everything we could
together. I hadn't wanted to find a best mate, in this place,
but now somehow here he was. And why not? I could sense
that the comradeship I'd draw from him could be the source
of a lot of strength, and I hoped I could help him in return.

ONE MORNING, JUST before 7 o'clock, our four-tonner
pulled up, its engine died and I slid out from under the
bench, rolled up my sleeping bag and jumped out into the
cold. The DS's instructions were as brief as they were
unpleasant: 'Right, get round fucking Dicky Bow Wood.'

Dicky Bow Wood. I'd heard about this place. It was named
for its figure-of-eight bow-tie shape and lies in the basin of
a valley. And it was tough. We'd pulled up less than a mile
away from it and I could see it down there – dark and wet
and foreboding. I took off, at first towards the front of the
group, but I quickly found myself falling back, and this time
it wasn't tactical. The day had hardly begun, and I was
already aching and tired. It was Afghanistan. I was suffering
for it. Whereas all the other guys had been looking after
themselves and getting in the practice, on the run-up to
Selection I'd been living in the desert, eating basic rations
and doing fourteen-hour patrols under stressful conditions.
I'd got into the habit of necking protein shakes, which were
helping a bit, but my body was beginning to feel distinctly

ragged. This wasn't an encouraging sign, on the second week of a six-month programme that's designed to get more brutal with every day that passes.

I finished that first go around Dicky Bow Wood panting, damp and anxious. We'd all found the DS waiting for us at the foot of a scree-covered hill that rose steeply over one hundred metres. Without letting us catch our breath he issued the next instruction: 'Grab whoever's closest to you and fireman's carry them up to the top.' Before I had the chance to see who was beside me, I felt a pair of cold hands grip the backs of my thighs and I was in the air, then over some shoulders. It was a lunk-headed giant from Redcar everyone knew as Crash. I knew why he'd chosen me: I was the shortest.

But I wasn't exactly light. Within minutes he was panting like an asthmatic hooker, dropping me into the muddy gravel every few metres before bundling me back up over his butcher's shoulders for another go. By the time we reached the top I was bruised and pissed off. For all the size of him, he had no stamina.

'Right!' shouted the DS. 'Get back down the fucking hill, then swap over.'

I looked at Crash in disbelief. Shit. I didn't even come up to his chin. How the fuck was I ...?

We reached the base of the hill. I bent down, threw my arms around the back of his legs and, with all the strength I could muster, hauled him on top of me. I felt like a blue whale had landed on my head. There was immediate and intense pressure on my knees, ankles and lower back. Now I had to get this sack of brawn up the hundred-metre hill. I pushed one leg out and then the next, with each step the weight shifting, bringing pain to a different part of my body. He was so huge, and the ascent so steep, that his head and legs kept banging along the ground.

And it wasn't only once. The DS ordered us up and down, up and down. By the fourth climb I felt like my eyes were going to pop. The only energy I had left was my anger. I stewed murderously, thinking, 'Fucking hell, you fat cunt. Why did you fucking choose me?' Halfway up the hill I was getting to the point where I didn't care whether I failed or not. I pushed on, my consciousness narrowing so that all there was left was the pain and what I could see directly in front of me – the mud, the scree and the toes of my boot. 'As long as you put one foot in front of the other, you'll get there,' I thought. On my fifth ascent I saw the man next to me give up, dropping his human load in a heap in the cold, chewed-up mud.

'What are you doing?' I shouted over to him.

'I can't do it,' he said.

'Where are you going? Just fucking walk up the hill.'

'I'm gone,' he said. 'I'm VW'ing.'

And from the misery of that man's defeat I squeezed just enough motivation to get me through.

* * *

WEEK TWO. FRIDAY. The Fan Dance. This is a test famous among the armed forces worldwide for its toughness – a timed march up Pen y Fan, the highest peak in southern Britain. Pen y Fan looks like a gigantic bat wing made of rock that rises nearly three thousand feet out of the earth. The route begins at the tip of one wing, and we'd have to tab over both shoulders and the head, then down the other side and back again, covering fifteen miles in three hours forty minutes.

The Selection nerds had been talking about the Fan Dance since they got here. They were convinced they knew the best strategy. I'd heard them every day telling each other, 'Just keep up with the DS and you'll pass. That's the secret. Just keep pace with them.' That, I'd decided, was a bad idea. As I paced briskly up the stony path with my fifty-five-pound bergen on my back and my weapon in my hands, I let one nerd after another overtake me, acknowledging each one's smug satisfaction. Fine. Go on, do it. Burn yourself out and I'll draw power from your flames.

And the truth was I needed all the power I could get. By the time I reached the centre of the ridge, the discomfort was rippling through every cell, as if my body was not made of flesh and blood anymore, but pain. I forced myself through the checkpoint and from then on it was downhill all the way. This was what they called Jacob's Ladder. It was by no means easier than going up. The ladder was almost vertical and strewn with rubble. One turn of the ankle and you'd be finished.

As I launched myself down the ladder I realised that, for once, my height was proving an advantage. I opened up my legs and let the heavy weight of my bergen take me, almost like controlled falling, keeping my knees bent so they wouldn't be punished too badly. I went like a firework, ticking off each one of the smug nerds as I rocketed down.

Finally, I was at the bottom. The Fan Dance had proved even more brutal than I'd feared. But here I was. I jogged, breathless and sodden in rain and sweat, down to the end of a cobbled track called the Roman Road, the vast black shadow of Pen y Fan looming over my shoulders. In the car park at the end there were eight or nine lads who'd arrived before me. One of the DS nodded me in.

'Right, take your bergen off, get a snack down you, drink some water.'

He handed me a packet of 'Biscuit Browns' – rock-hard squares made of wheat that are notorious for giving you constipation and have since been removed from army ration packs.

'Thanks, sir,' I said. I ripped open the gold foil packet.

'OK, lads,' the DS shouted. 'You've got five minutes. Then you're doing it again.'

How was this even possible? I sat down on the edge of a rock and chewed my dry mouthful in a daze. Around me I could see some of the other guys were having a serious mental battle with themselves. Their eyes were just detached from reality, as if their spirit had been sucked out of their bodies and was looking down on them from high above. The idea of doing it again, when they'd used their last whisper of strength to even get here, seemed like nothing more than a joke. They could barely walk another step, let alone dance the fan. They just sat there in silence, feeling the rain on their cheeks, trying not to think at all.

Just then, the DS emerged from where he'd disappeared around the back of a wagon. In one hand, he was holding a steaming mug of tea. In the other, a large plate piled high with Fondant Fancies and Cherry Bakewells. He stood in the middle of us, slurped his tea loudly and, with an exaggerated flourish, took a huge bite out of a bright pink Fancy.

'Hmm, that's bloody good,' he said, letting us all have a good look at the airy blonde sponge and the sweet, creamy filling.

It filled my vision, like it was a delicious swimming pool I was about to dive into.

'There's plenty more cake and tea round the back of the wagon, lads,' said the DS.

He shoved the rest of it into his mouth and swallowed theatrically. 'Why are you doing this to yourselves? Come on. You can end this misery now with a click of your fingers. Just stand up and come for some tea and cake. Simple as.'

I looked at my boots, the dark wet mud and the green shreds of vegetation clinging to the leather. I balled my fist, feeling my fingertips push into my palms, feeling the strange machinery of tendons and gristle beneath them. Somewhere above me a crow took off from the branch of a tree. To my left I heard a rustle, followed by a deep sigh. Someone was standing up. We all watched him walk to the back of the van to have his chinwag with Mr Kipling. Then someone else stood up. Then someone else. It was a domino effect. I couldn't believe it.

But I welcomed it. I pushed myself to my feet and I was gone.

BY THE LAST week of the Hills, we'd lost more than half the course, and there wasn't a man remaining that didn't feel ragged. Each one of us now had five hundred arduous miles in our legs and, not having had the benefit of a proper preparation, I was really feeling it. As we bounced along the dirt track towards the start of the next challenge I knew the disadvantage I was carrying from Sangin was going to show itself at some point. What I didn't know was when or how.

Today was yet another weighted march, this one with fifty-five pounds plus food, water and weapon for fifteen miles along the Elan Valley in the Brecon Beacons. The trouble finally arrived after I'd hit my first checkpoint, in the form of an unusually dense fog. Within seconds I could see almost nothing at all. It was completely disorientating, like running through milk. I felt the panic rise from my stomach and expand into my whole body. In my exhausted state I didn't have the mental energy to fight it.

'Just keep going on your compass bearing,' I told myself out loud. 'Just keep going.' But the deeper I vanished into the fog, the more I began to doubt myself. Was I going in the right direction? Was I sure? I stopped, utterly alone inside a silent world of cloud, and tried to think. 'Be on the safe side,' I said. 'Go back to where you were before the clag came in.' I turned around and began retracing my steps. After about two hundred metres I realised I didn't recognise the terrain at all. I looked at my map. Where was I? *Where was I?* I had no idea. Which meant I was going to miss the next check-point. Which meant I was going to fail Selection.

As the reality dawned, my heartbeat surged and my breath began pumping in shallow bellows. 'I'm fucked,' I thought. 'I'm going to have to call the fucking RAF in to come and get me. I'm going to have to call in Search and Rescue. What's Emilie going to say? What's Darren going to think? I've failed. This is it. It's over. I'm done.'

In that instant my entire sense of who I was just fell away. I'd made a mistake, and that mistake became who I was in my entirety. It defined me. It was me. I felt like a fraud, like I didn't deserve to be on Selection at all. My mind was telling me, 'I'm not what I think I am. I'm not what I believed I could be. I've bitten off far more than I can chew. I should just be in a unit as a gunner.' If there had been a button to press where I could fail myself, I would have pressed it.

This is something I've witnessed happening time and again, not only on Selection, not only in the military, but in

195

every environment I've ever operated in. It's not the mistake that makes people fail, it's the psychological effects of having made that mistake in the first place. We all like to think of ourselves as immune from making errors. But if we're too much in denial of the fact that they're inevitable, when the truth hits we're panicked into believing all the worst things about ourselves. It's as if the mistake has remoulded us into the person everyone who ever dismissed or derided us thought we were. It triggers a cascade effect that makes us panic, then despair and then, finally, give up. When that cascade happens, we've allowed the mistake to possess us. We've allowed it to win.

There was a classic example of exactly this process on Series 3 of *SAS: Who Dares Wins*. Contestant number six had stood out from the very beginning of filming, and mostly in good ways. He was a gym-fit lad with a positive mindset who'd come from a really rough background in Middlesbrough. He had the right attitude to succeed. He was taking it seriously, but not so seriously that he couldn't have a laugh at himself – and that's crucial. When you're in the shit you've got to be able to stand outside yourself and have a chuckle at your situation, otherwise it'll all get on top of you. He was at the top of the intake, the man most likely to win.

We soon learned that he'd experienced some pretty tricky situations in his life. At some point he'd got into serious debt with drug dealers and had to turn to his parents to bail him out, which they could ill afford to do. It was when he was talking about all this that I got my first niggle about him. He'd really dragged his family through the shit and didn't seem that bothered by it.

'So you're not worried that you put your mum and dad through all this stress?' I asked.

'It's been a struggle, but I'm in a good place now,' he said, smiling, bringing the discussion straight back to himself.

There was no emotion there. He seemed unfazed about what he'd done to his family. Almost selfish. He was still living with his mum and dad, and was acting as if that was the way things should be – that their entire purpose in life was to look after him.

That evening, while the contestants were all at dinner, we started digging into his personal life. All the contestants put on a façade when they come on the show. In order to get at them psychologically, it's essential that we get a sense of the real person. For that, social media is a goldmine. You can more or less grab a complete picture of someone's social and family life from just pictures and words. We checked out his Instagram, his Facebook, his Twitter. And then, on LinkedIn, we struck gold.

Later on, just as everyone was relaxing, I sent the order for him to be delivered to the Mirror Room. He was called for, hooded and walked through the usual disorientation drills, after which he found himself sitting opposite me and Billy. When his hood came off, he was his usual chirpy self.

'You all right?' he said.

'Yeah!' I said, beaming back at him, as if we were old friends. 'Mate, you never fucking told us you were one of the boys.'

He looked confused.

'Talk to me about the Parachute Regiment,' I said, turning the laptop towards him. 'Obviously a big part of your life. Your CV's quite impressive. I like that.'

As soon as he saw what was on the screen, he mentally left the room. His mind went somewhere else. In front of me and Billy was just a pale shell, staring.

'Welcome to the brotherhood!' said Billy. 'We're brothers. You know that, don't you? What battalion were you in?'

'If I'm honest, Staff,' he said, 'it's a lie, Staff.'

I slammed the table with my fist and got straight to my feet, my chair crashing back behind me.

'You fucking lying little cunt,' I said, inches from his face.

He tried to speak.

'Shut the fuck up,' I shouted.

'Have you heard of stolen valour?' said Billy. 'Friends of mine have fucking died to be called a paratrooper. Gave their fucking blood.'

When his bollocking was finally over, we shouted for the guard and let him stew for the night.

First thing in the morning, we lined up the contestants and began a mile-long run down to where the first task was taking place.

'After today, we move on to the next stage of the course,' I told them as we ran. 'And believe you me, I'm not taking half of you. Fifty per cent are getting culled, tonight, because you haven't made the grade. You could save yourselves a lot of pain and leave right now if you want. Just think about that, because when we get to where we're going, you're going to be in a whole world of pain, for a couple of hours at least.'

This little speech was mostly for the benefit of number six. The truth was, we had no intention of culling him. Everyone makes mistakes, and his hadn't even been made on the course. This was a test. I wanted to see if he was going to allow his mistake to eat him alive.

We soon arrived at the flood plain of a river, now a field of thick mud on which we'd marked out a murder ball pitch with a large tyre in the middle. Number six didn't even say anything. He came straight up to me and took his armband off.

'What you giving me that for?' I asked him. 'I don't want it.'

'Well …'

'Are you sure you want to give me that?'

He handed it to me.

'Are you sure you want to give me that?'

'Yeah.'

And off he went.

He hadn't even tried to fight his way through that mistake. Instead, he'd been through the classic cascade: panic, despair, surrender. In a way I could sympathise. I'd been only too lucky that giving up simply wasn't an option in the Elan Valley. Instead, I had to force myself back under control. 'Calm yourself down, Ant,' I'd said, speaking aloud. 'You know you're a good soldier. You know you're good at map reading. You've just made a mistake. Yes, you could fail the course. But you need to get yourself out of this.'

I reckoned that I'd probably gone off track for about a mile. I walked back down the hill, trying to orientate myself. I didn't recognise anything. Now the fog had lifted a little, I could see only endless grass and mud and scree, the tufts of thick grass they call babies heads, the bogs filled with freezing brown water. I realised, now, why everyone calls this place 'the green desert'.

Finally, I glimpsed what looked like the brow of a hill. I ran to the top to get a look around and saw, about fifty metres away, a little stream. 'Yes!' I thought. I opened the map again so I could try and zone in on my whereabouts using the stream as a landmark. My heart sinking, I realised there were waterways like this everywhere – dozens of them. The blue streams on the map looked like veins on a tea-lady's leg. I ran down to the river and followed it. After about fifteen minutes I found a Y junction. 'Yes!' I shouted, practically falling to my knees with gratitude. This was a feature I'd be able to place on the map. I found it, took a bearing from it and was back on my way. But I wasn't out of trouble yet. I was at least half an hour late. And if I didn't finish on time, I'd be failed.

By the last leg of the march I was absolutely hanging out, my muscles were trying to go into spasm, my will was almost empty and my feet were mangled, puffed and bloody, feeling for all the world like lumps of gnawed meat hanging off the end of my legs. I was also panicking. We were forbidden from wearing watches, so I had no idea how late I was running. At the top of a hill I saw the checkpoint and the DS there. I squinted down. Yes! He was still checking men through. I was still in time, just about, but I knew the DS could stop and pack in at any second. Overwhelmed, I put my weapon against the fence post, leapt over and charged down the hill.

I'd made it. But then, just as I thought I was through, the DS stopped me. And he didn't look happy.

'Middleton,' he said.

'Yes, staff?'

'Why did you take both hands off your weapon at the top of the hill? You're meant to have two hands on your weapon at all times.'

I couldn't believe he'd seen me up there. It was like he had some sort of sixth sense. How the fuck? But there was no way I could give him any bullshit.

'I've got no excuse, staff,' I said.

He opened his flip pad that had a little rain jacket on it and made a note.

'Take your bergen off,' he said.

I did as he asked. He pulled the scales towards him and lifted my pack onto it. There was a silence.

'What's wrong with your bergen, Middleton?' he asked.

I looked at the scales. I couldn't believe it. There was no way. It was impossible. My bergen was two pounds light.

'It's underweight, staff.'

'Correct,' he said. 'Get in the wagon.'

I pulled myself up to find Darren sitting in there on the bench, a stew of sweat and dirt ground into his face. I didn't have to say a word. He could see that I was crushed.

'What's wrong, lad?' he said.

'DS saw me take my hands off my weapon,' I said, 'and my fucking bergen's under.'

'It's under?'

The sheer shock on his face was a reminder I didn't need about how serious this was.

'It'll be all right,' he said, thinly. 'Try not to bother your-self with it.'

But I wasn't listening. I had my head between my knees, just drowning out the sound.

'They're going to think I'm a cheat,' I said. 'How the fuck has this happened?'

Then it clicked. Of course! I'd forgotten to take my protein shake out of my bag before I'd weighed it that morning. Then, during the march, I'd drunk the shake and that two pounds was the difference. Not that there was any point explaining this to the directing staff. Excuses were worthless here. I just had to suck it up and accept that I was about to be failed.

That night, I nervously approached the noticeboard in the galley that listed the men who'd passed and their times. I ran my finger down the sheet of paper, my heart thumping in my chest. There I was … and there was a red card next to my name. But I felt as much fury as I did relief. I'd let myself down, that day. One more error and it was all over.

The final test of the Hills is known as the 'Long Drag'. It's a weighted run over the Brecon Beacons that we were required to navigate ourselves, using a compass and map to get to various checkpoints in allotted times. We had to cover forty miles with seventy pounds on our backs, carrying our weapon, and we had to do it in twenty hours. Most people either went on the top of the hill or took the route that lay down in the valley. I decided to contour it, pacing one foot in front of the other along the ridge lines of a steep hill for miles. It put huge pressure on my ankles, tracking for miles on the edge of a goat track, constantly on the slope, never stopping for more than five minutes because I didn't want to get demoralised in the freezing mud and needle-sharp rain. My right ankle took the brunt and became so sore I kind of went out the other side of it, and was only aware of a very distant burst of pain, like a star exploding in a far-off galaxy. Knowing that I'd highlighted myself so badly, I'd become possessed by a kind of angry desperation. I found myself in a trance state. I was just going and going, almost trying to punish myself for my error.

When I was, I guessed, about two hours away from the finish I saw a checkpoint at the bottom of a hill. I pressed on towards it, girding myself for the agonising final push beyond it. But when I got there, the DS stopped me again.

'Right, Middleton,' he said. 'You're all done.'

'I'm done? I don't understand, staff.'

'Take your bergen off and get in the wagon.'

'In the wagon, staff?' I said.

I didn't know what was happening. I had maybe three miles to go before I finished, so what the fuck had I done wrong? 'Is this a game?' I thought. 'Are they trying to fuck me over?' I cautiously did as I was asked and pulled myself up into the four-tonner. A couple of the lads were already in the back. They looked surprised to see me.

'Ant, I thought I left you near the back?' said one.

'I went a different way,' I said. 'I contoured it.'

'Fuckin' nice one.'

'Mate, is this for real?' I said. 'This is the end? They're not playing with us?'

'Ant,' he laughed. 'What you going on about? You fucking smashed it.'

LEADERSHIP LESSONS

Never allow the mistake to win. We all make them. It's allowing that mistake to take you over that's the real problem. When you make a mistake you should accept that it's happened, push all the self-recriminations aside and calmly make a new plan.

Don't be intimidated by all the people you have to beat to get to the top. It was a dizzying moment for me, in Sennybridge, when I saw the amount of bodies in that room, knowing that only a handful would pass. The numbers are irrelevant. The only thing that counts is you.

Don't listen to the know-it-alls. You'll always encounter people who are utterly convinced they know everything there is to know about the task ahead and want the world to know about it too. These are exactly the people you should be cautious of. The smart people in the room aren't the ones giving it out – they're the ones taking it all in.

THE WAR IS ALWAYS IN YOUR HEAD

'WHAT'S HAPPENED TO my bed?' I thought. 'Why's it so uncomfortable tonight?'

I stirred, trying for what seemed like the thousandth time to get comfortable. Unable to do so, I opened my eyes a crack. All the lights were on. That was weird. Where was Emilie? Why was I wearing these nasty thin tracksuit bottoms? I opened my eyes fully and propped myself up on an elbow. And then it all came back to me in a terrible flood. I was in a cell somewhere in the bowels of Chelmsford Police Station. And 'bowels' was right – for I was deep in the shit.

Soon I heard the door rattling and clanking before finally whining open. A middle-aged police officer with a bald head appeared on the other side of it.

'How are you this morning, Mr Middleton?'

'Could murder a cup of tea.'

'Any injuries?'

'Well, my head's fucking pounding.'

'Need to see a doctor?'

'No, mate, I'm fine.'

'Well, your solicitor's here.'

'Solicitor?' I said. 'I haven't called any solicitor.'

'Well, someone's called him in,' he said. 'You got any mates know you're here? Anyway, come on. Up and 'ave it. He's waiting for you.'

I rubbed my eyes and stood.

I'd been out of the military for six months, having completed two successful tours of Afghanistan with the SBS. Going straight into responsible daily life as a husband, provider and father on civvy street had not been easy. As tough as military life can be, what it gives you is a structure and a routine. It's like having a drill sergeant constantly living with you, telling you where you need to be, what you need to do and when to go to bed. When that suddenly vanishes, after you've spent most of your adult life relying on it, it's not unusual for ex-servicemen to feel disorientated. Some get depressed. Some turn to drink. Some lash out in violence. Some end up homeless or even in prison. I'd managed to find some work, here and there, on the security circuit, but nothing permanent. For the first time in years I had no goal to set my sights on, no Everest to climb. I didn't think it was affecting me too badly. Turns out I was wrong.

The police officer led me down an echoing corridor to a small interview room. Sitting waiting for me were two other officers and my solicitor, who was someone I knew from Chelmsford. On the table was a small portable TV monitor. After some not-very-pleasantries, one of the police officers switched on the screen and pressed play on the recorder. It was the CCTV footage from the previous night.

I'd been reconnecting with some of my old mates. Ten of us had met in Chelmsford town centre at 6 o'clock on a Sunday evening and we'd bounced from The Toad to Edwards to Lloyds to the Yates's, ending up at Chicago's nightclub. We'd blagged a large table in the corner to settle into, ordering bottles of vodka and Jack Daniel's with jugs of Coca-Cola and cranberry juice to be delivered to our table. We'd probably drunk our way through about £600 already.

At just after 1 a.m. some of my pals went out for a smoke. I was pouring myself a fresh vodka and watching the dance-floor going up to 'I've got the Power' by Snap when I became aware of someone running towards me.

'Ant,' he said. 'Mate. It's all kicking off outside.'

We pushed our way through the sticky, leery bodies and out into the cold street. I didn't know what situation I was about to meet exactly, but I wasn't worried. After surviving suicide bombers and AK-47-wielding Taliban thugs in the darkest hellpits of Afghanistan, I thought I could handle a few wallies outside an Essex nightclub.

Out on the pavement I discovered that three women had started an argument with one of my friends. They were jabbing fingers at him, telling him to go fuck himself. He, of course, was returning this in kind. I pushed my way in between them.

'Oi! Oi! Oi!' I said. 'Take it down a notch. Calm it down. Come on.'

I put my arm around the pal who was at the centre of the row and began walking him in the direction of the taxi rank. As I was manoeuvring him away from the scene, I turned to the women. 'And you lot, fuck off,' I said.

I came back to find that the three women had not fucked off. Instead, they'd been joined by their male friends. The rest of my pals had now piled in properly, and the shouting had taken on a new and dangerous intensity. This, I realised, was seconds away from turning into a full-on street brawl. I started grabbing my friends, one by one, and putting them into taxis, all under a hail of abuse from the idiots. They were about half gone when two police officers arrived. 'Thank God,' I thought. 'Back-up. At last.'

I knew from my training with the Met at Hendon that the first move law enforcement are supposed to make in a situation like this is to separate the fighting parties. If they're no longer able to make contact with each other, the abuse stops and the trouble rapidly de-escalates. Nine times out of ten it's the magic bullet that kills the aggression.

I carried on clearing my pals into cabs as the officers approached the women. I was expecting them to move them on, but for some reason they didn't. They just stood there with them, allowing them to continue hurling abuse. I tried to ignore it, and had just put the last man in a cab, when the woman at the front, who'd kicked it all off, started insulting me.

'You silly fucking cunt,' she said. 'What are you? A babysitter? Do you change their fucking nappies an' all? Fucking prick.'

Now I was getting angry. I turned to the male officer, who was just standing there, his hands in his pockets, with a silly, nervous grin on his face.

'Why don't you take them round the corner rather than leaving them here, gobbing off?'

'Who the fuck do you think you're talking to?' he said.

'Don't get all attitude with me.' I walked towards him. 'I'm the one that's defused the situation.'

Suddenly, he was up in my face.

'You need to go home now,' he said.

'Just answer me one question,' I said. 'Why are they still here? I'm doing your job for you and you're stood there with them doing nothing. Move them five metres down the road and they've got no one to abuse.'

He stretched his finger out and poked me in the middle of the chest. I can't remember what he was saying, because by now everything was darkening and narrowing and stretching out. I looked down at what he was doing.

'You want to watch what you're doing with that finger,' I said. It happened in slow motion. He jabbed me again, this time hard between the ribs. Its force pushed me back slightly.

Before my body had had the chance to right itself, my fist had made impact with his jaw.

He was on the pavement. Flat. Sprawled. Silent. To my left, I saw the female officer reach for her CS gas. She blasted me with it. I turned and blocked the spray with one arm. As I was doing so, the officer beneath me roused and tried to stagger to his feet, while grabbing for his cosh. In his semi-conscious daze he tumbled back into a shop window. As he flailed about, trying to regain his balance, I took a step towards him, grabbed fistfuls of his uniform with both hands, lifted him off the ground, raised him up and slammed him back down. He landed on the pavement with a thud. He didn't move. I pulled the cosh from his hand. For just a second I had the strange sensation of stepping out of my body and looking down at the scene: there was me, crouched over an unconscious police officer. And there, in my hand, was a cosh. 'This,' I thought, 'does not look good.'

I ran.

My footsteps echoed along a narrow, empty street. Within seconds it sounded as if the whole of Chelmsford had gone up with the cat's-cry of sirens. The police must have been watching it all on CCTV, and by now they'd had enough time to leap into their cars and vans and flood the town centre. I took a left and a right, making the most of my knowledge of the back lanes, stopping briefly beside a drain, down which I posted the cosh. The sirens seemed to be getting louder. The walls of the buildings around me flashed blue. I took off, only for the slap-slap-slap of my trainers hitting the ground to be joined by the thud of boots. I was being chased. I nipped down an alleyway and turned a corner, hoisted myself over an eight-foot wall and landed into a crouch. I waited, in total silence, not even letting the sound of my breathing betray my position. They passed by.

The sirens were so loud they'd become deafening, like something out of the Blitz. I crept forwards, cat-like, peering up, trying to see where the CCTV cameras were. As far as I could tell there were none back here. But I had a problem. In front of me there was only one way I could go: the River Can. I moved towards it, keeping low in the shadows. The water was black and deep, and an icy, metallic breeze whipped off it. The far shore was a good twenty feet away. I'd have to swim it. I bent down and dipped my fingers under the choppy surface. It was freezing. I had no choice.

I put one foot in and then the other. The river filled my trainers. Lowering myself down, I felt the level of the water's surface rise up my body in a line of crackling, numbing pain. When I was up to my shoulders I pushed myself into the middle of the river, my toes quickly losing touch with the river bed. I told myself to be careful – the River Can was no doubt littered with several decade's worth of shopping trolleys and other hazards. There was a chance I could get tangled up and stuck.

In the streets above me sirens blared and vehicles tore about. It felt oddly quiet and separate down here in the water, as if all the commotion were happening in a faraway place that wasn't quite real. To my right I saw an arched footbridge and, underneath that, clinging to the bank, a large, dark bush. It gave me an idea. Rather than swim across to the other bank, and most likely directly into the arms of a waiting officer, I'd glide over there and just wait it out. As I made a silent breaststroke down the river, the freezing water lapped against my chin. My fingers were turning numb and my feet were being dragged down by the weight of my socks and shoes, but before long I was there.

I don't know how long I waited underneath that bush, gripping on to the chains above that lined the pathway, with only my head above water. The ruckus above me echoed noisily as the numbing spread and my body became heavier and heavier. They seemed to be zeroing in on my location, somehow. Somewhere in the upper world I heard a voice.

'Where the hell is he?'

'He can't have gone far.'

'You'd hope. Who knows?'

'The dogs would find him. Are they on the way?'

'Not sure.' There was a silence. 'Should we call them in?'

'Yeah, reckon. Get hold of Mike, would you?'

'OK, Sarge.'

Less than five minutes later I heard the slamming of van doors and the animals above my head, barking, sniffing, claws clattering on the ground. I lowered my head into the river as far as it would go, leaving only the tip of my nose, my eyes and forehead above the surface. They didn't seem to be having much joy up there. Despite my discomfort, my spirits rose. I knew that being down here in the water was ideal for avoiding having them pick up my scent.

The crackle of a radio. 'Go ahead?' said a woman on the bridge. She listened for a moment. 'Hey, guys, hang on – someone's said they saw him go into the water and no one's seen him get out of it again.'

There was a silence.

'Let's get the dive team in,' said someone else. 'And tell them to get on with it, yeah? If he's in there, and we can't see him, there's a chance he's at the bottom of it, or will be soon. What was he wearing? Do we know?'

'T-shirt and jeans.'

'Really? T-shirt and jeans? Oh, he's fucked then.'

Down in the water I noticed the surface of the river around me had started vibrating. I was wondering what was causing it, then suddenly realised it was me. I was violently shivering. I'd been under that bush for at least twenty minutes by now, and my jaw was starting to lock. This, I knew, was the onset of hypothermia. I watched help-lessly as the juddering of my body sent more and more ripples out onto the surface of the river in rapidly expand-ing circles.

'Here, Ian! Look down there,' said the woman's voice. 'Do you see that?'

'What?'

'Those ripples on the water. Can you see?'

There was a silence.

'What, those?'

'Yeah! The ripples! Is that him? Is he under the bridge?'

I could see, in the dark reflection on the water's surface, two police officers bending over the side of the bridge. I was done. It was over. I pushed myself off from the bank and floated out into the middle, right underneath where they were looking, and trod water.

'Good evening officers,' I said. 'Is there something I can help you with?'

'Get the fuck out of that fucking river now or you're going to get fucking tasered,' said the guy.

'You're going to taser me in the water?' I said. 'Are you absolutely sure about that?'

'Just get out,' he said.

'I'm obviously under arrest, I get that,' I said. 'But if I get out of this and you start fucking pissing me off and roughing me up, I'm going to start up a whole new feud. I'm warning you.'

At the riverbank one of the policemen gave me a hand up and hauled me out.

'You're under arrest on suspicion of assaulting a police officer,' he said. 'You do not have to say anything but it may harm your defence if you do not mention when questioned something which you later rely on in court. Anything you do say may be given in evidence.'

Ten minutes later I was shivering in the back of the police van, handcuffs around my wrists, four space blankets draped over my shoulders.

And that was my Sunday night.

BACK IN THE interview room the officer pressed pause on the remote control. There I was, on the little screen, crouched over an unconscious policeman with a cosh in my hand.

'That is me,' I nodded. 'I did do that. I'll put my hands up.'

I just wanted to get out of there as quickly as possible. Whatever they had decided to do with me – fine me, issue me a caution – as long as they hurried up about it, I didn't really mind.

Half an hour later, when I finally stepped out of Chelmsford police station into that grim, milky-skied morning, the most immediate thing on my mind was coffee. My solicitor took me to a nearby Costa and we sat in the window with large lattes as I tried to get my head around exactly what had just happened.

'I thought ...' I said, rubbing my temples. 'I was expecting a fine. A caution. I can't believe it. What are they charging me with again?'

'Actual bodily harm against the male officer and common assault against the female.'

'Common assault?' I said. 'That is so much bullshit. I didn't lay a finger on her. How can that be assault?'

'I'm afraid that's how it goes these days,' he said. 'If you spit at someone, that's common assault. If you swear at them, it's common assault. You don't have to make physical contact with them. If you do anything that makes them fear for their personal safety, that's an assault.'

'But she's a police officer,' I said. 'No one should be attacked, I get that, but isn't what happened to her last night just part of the everyday job? If she can't even handle standing one metre away from a little ruck between two guys, then she's not qualified to be on the force. She should be on the tills in Waitrose, not out on the streets.'

'I didn't say I agreed with it,' he said. 'It's just how it goes these days.'

I picked up my coffee and looked out of the window, scowling. My clothes were still wet from the river, my trainers sodden.

'This fucking society nowadays, everyone's so protected,' I said. 'They're mollycoddled. They're wrapped up in cotton wool. Even the coppers. It's a blame culture. It's pathetic.'

'And I'm afraid, Ant, that it's also common assault. But don't worry. It's not a particularly serious charge. And we have a very strong case that there are good mitigating circumstances. You were trying to stop the trouble, not start it. And someone with your military service?'

'I put my hand up for it, too,' I said, nodding. 'That's got to count for something.' I sat forward, suddenly rallying.

'You know what? We should hit that policeman with abuse of authority charges. In his statement he claimed he'd grabbed hold of me because he was fearing for his safety. But I know from my time at Hendon that if you fear for your safety, you're taught never to grab hold of someone. You're supposed to step back and put your arm up. If you're really in fear, you put your cosh out, extend it and use it in a defensive position. You don't start jabbing someone in the chest. So let's go after him.'

The solicitor sighed. 'That's going to cost a bit of money. And tactically, it might not be the wisest move.'

I glanced out of the window again. Along the other side of the street I saw a guy I used to know from the gym. He was walking his wife's miniature pug. He was wearing pink trainers and had his hair tied up in a bun. What was this world I'd come back to?

'Maybe it's best not to aggravate the situation with the police,' I said.

'Don't worry,' he said. 'Most likely outcome? You're looking at a couple of years suspended.'

It would be nine months before my final reckoning. During that time the charge of ABH had been elevated to GBH because the police officer claimed he'd suffered permanent damage to his eye. It sounded bad, but my solicitor felt sure that the significant mitigating circumstances, combined with my military record, meant the most likely outcome would be me getting off with a suspended sentence.

When the day came, we all took our places in the miserable brick fortress that is Chelmsford Crown Court. With Emilie and her dad watching on, my barrister argued that the incident amounted to nothing more than 'a mild altercation that turned into a fight between two men'.

But the prosecution pushed back. 'There was no fight,' they said. 'The only fight that night was coming from Mr Middleton.'

Then they played the CCTV footage. The judge leaned forward, squinting at the screen, watching the build-up on the street outside the nightclub. 'Who is that peacekeeper in the middle, there?' he asked. 'The one splitting the groups up?'

My barrister pumped up his chest and announced with booming gravitas, 'That, your honour, is my client, Anthony Middleton.'

It was a fantastic moment. It could only mean good news. As the proceedings wound on, I began slowly allowing myself to relax. Eventually, it was time for the judge's summing up. The moment he fixed me with his bird-of-prey eyes I knew things had somehow taken a terrible turn.

'You are a highly trained and experienced former Special Forces operator,' he said. 'You should have known better.'

He handed me down a sentence of twenty-six months in prison, with six months taken off for pleading guilty at the earliest opportunity and another six due to my character references. That left fourteen months inside. Across the courtroom, Emilie was sitting in the gallery with her dad. Both of them looked pale and shocked.

'I love you,' I called out to her. 'It'll be all right.'

'I love you too,' she said, visibly gathering herself together. 'We've got this.'

That was all I needed to hear. The moment I broke eye contact with her I was in the zone. There was no anger anymore. No shock. No self-pity. No negativity. This was prison. There was nothing I could do about it but dive in head first. I was led out of the court by two members of the prison staff and put into the back of a transport van. They locked me into a tiny cubicle and I was driven to Chelmsford Prison. I didn't look out of the window. That world, out there, of shops and music and sunlight was nothing to do with me anymore. As we drove, for a horrible moment I almost felt I might drown in the shame I was feeling at what I'd done to my family. I squeezed my eyes and clenched my fists. I had to get hold of myself. There was no other choice.

As we made halting progress through the Chelmsford traffic I tried to marshal my thoughts. My overwhelming concern was that I'd end up fighting. There was no way I could let people walk over me in there. There was no question that I had to defend myself. But what would happen if and when there was physical violence? If I flipped out, I knew I'd probably cause some serious damage. My goal was obviously to be let out early for good behaviour, but that kind of trouble could see me being kept inside for years. Not for the first time, I realised that this was going to be more of a mental game than a physical one. My most dangerous enemy would be myself. This war would be fought inside my head.

When the wagon pulled up I was led, along with a young lad of around eighteen, into a reception building. Our personal possessions were confiscated and sealed up in plastic bags, then I was taken into a side room, stripped and made to squat, so they could check I wasn't smuggling anything inside me. If they thought they were going to humiliate me or make me feel in any way ashamed by making me do this, they didn't know me very well. I stood up, my mind a machine, and collected my allotted prison gear: two plain T-shirts, two grey tracksuit bottoms, two grey jumpers, plimsolls and bed sheets.

In yet another small room we were processed by a 'trusted' inmate, a scrawny-looking guy with a wispy blond beard hanging off his chin who handed us both what looked like credit cards.

'These are your telephone cards,' he said. 'Guard them with your life.' Then came a small pile of papers. 'These are your canteen sheets. I'll show you how to fill them out in a bit. On this sheet you'll find all your timings – that's when you eat, when you get locked in your cell, when all your roll call times are.'

I glanced down it.

'You have to make sure you're stood by your door at eight in the morning,' he continued. 'Breakfast is at eight thirty.

You've got half an hour to eat, then you're back to your cell to get banged up again. They let you out for lunch at half twelve, then you get banged up again at one.'

'Fun,' I said, folding the paper away. I turned to the kid next to me.

'Are you all right?' He gave me an insincere nod. 'You'll be fine,' I reassured him, although the truth was I really wasn't sure.

Wizard-chin led us down a wide corridor and into a holding area that had an old table and a couple of couches in it that smelled of bleach and sweat. More trusted inmates were hanging about in there, for no obvious reason, all dressed in their regulation light grey at-Her-Majesty's-leisurewear. I was aware of them trying to subtly check us over with furtive glances, while not breaking their conversation. It wasn't long before one of them slouched over and sat himself chummily on the arm of the couch.

'All right, mate,' he grinned, scratching his boney, yellowish arm. He looked over our piles of clothing. 'You got everything you need?'

'Yes, mate,' I said. 'Thanks for asking.'

'They give you your phone card yet?' he said.

'Got it,' I nodded.

'Sweet,' he said. 'Chuck us it here and I'll show you how to use it.'

'No, mate. I'm happy that I know how to use it,' I said. 'I've been told.'

'I'm a trusted inmate, yeah?' he said. 'Give us it here. Come on. I want to show you something.'

I stared ahead. When he realised I wasn't giving in, he stood and got in front of me. There was dried spittle on the edges of his lips and he had one of those mouths that show more gum than teeth. He had crust in the corners of his eyes and his skin had an almost greenish pallor.

'Mate,' he said, trying to act the tough guy. 'I told you to give it here.'

I could destroy this prick in less than a second. I wouldn't even have to get out of my seat.

'And I told you,' I said. 'I've got my card. I know how to use it. Thank you very much, though. I appreciate the kind offer of help.'

From the other side of the room another inmate piped up. 'You lot,' he said. 'Keep the fucking noise down, will you?'

That was it. I was up.

'Am I fucking talking too loud, mate?' I said. 'I'm fucking talking too loud, am I?'

'No, mate,' he said. 'You're all right.'

'Be careful who you talk to, because you don't fucking know me and you don't want to fucking know me.' I turned to the other one. Before I had the chance to say any more, he'd shrunk back.

'All right, mate, no worries.'

I returned to my place on the couch, waiting to be led to my cell. I couldn't believe what had just happened. Was it going to be like this every day? How was I going to keep a lid on it? How was I going to stop myself breaking someone's jaw?

Finally, a prison officer arrived and we were led out into a huge indoor courtyard. Around us was a massive horseshoe of cells and windows, three storeys high. Voices echoed out above our heads – 'Fresh meat!' 'Oooh! Oooh! Oooh!' 'I'm gonna fuck you up.' The young lad beside me was pale and was clutching his gear to his chest. I looked up in the direction of the Fresh Meat cell, thinking, 'I would so love to come to your cell right now and knock on the door.' I was thankful to discover I'd been given a cell of my own. Once inside I took my shoes off, put them neatly by the door, and lay back on the mattress. It was so thin and ragged it immediately brought to mind my days as a craphat back in Aldershot.

The next morning all the inmates had to step outside their cells for roll call. I made sure I was present and correct at 8 o'clock as a prison officer checked us all off on his clipboard. I glanced to my left. Standing beside me was an obvious drug addict. He had no teeth, his clothes were stained with cum and tea, and he stank. I looked to my right. There was a man who was inside for burgling houses. The prison officer doing the roll call was viewing me as if I were no different from them. And I wasn't. I was just a prisoner number too. If anything, I was worse. Most of these wretches had started out with nothing. But me? I'd had a beautiful wife and family, and a prestigious job that I loved. I'd had everything I ever wanted, and I'd lost it.

For the first time in years I was glad my dad wasn't around. I thought of him often, as the days in prison turned to weeks. Looking back upon my life up to now, I realised that the military had, in many ways, taken over my dad's role. It had given me structure, it had taught me how to behave, it had given me a goal to reach for and rules to kick against, to find out who I was. Now I'd left all that behind me, and what had happened? I'd crumbled. After everything I'd achieved and lived through, was I still not man enough to be out there, in the world, alone? Could I not control myself? Could I not fight that war in my head and win?

As the weeks ground on I managed to get into a routine. I'd spend my time keeping my cell immaculate, sweeping it out twice a day and making my bed properly. But, just like when I was in Afghanistan, I made a conscious decision not to make my personal space homely. Some inmates had nice rugs in their spaces and candles and pictures of the family. Mine was just an empty cell with a bed and toilet. I wasn't going to try and kid myself that this was anywhere I could feel comfortable. This was prison. It was a negative place. I didn't belong here. Full stop.

But I also knew that if I was to avoid flipping out and hurting someone, I'd have to find a way of not getting sucked into that negativity. I tried to focus my mind on all the things I wanted to do after my release. I worked out in the gym and took on as many jobs as they'd let me do. I served food. I was a cleaner, mopping floors while everyone else was asleep. Soon I was also given permission to leave my cell between seven and eight at night, and teach inmates to read and write. I was shocked to discover how many of them couldn't even do the basics. It brought it home that, at heart, a lot of these guys weren't bad people; they just hadn't been given the tools to properly survive in the world.

I also had another advantage. There were a few people inside that I either already knew personally or had direct connections with from pals in Essex. I know what it sounds like, but there's no other way of really putting it: some of my friends are gangsters. I'm not talking about petty crime gangs, either. These are top boys from top firms, the kind of men whose names get whispered around the bazaars. I started hanging around with one in particular, who was a former member of the Royal Green Jackets, an infantry regiment of the British Army. He did a lot of heavy work – collection, intimidation – for a top East End gang but had got caught with a commercial quantity of drugs on him. We swapped war stories. He told me about the drugs deals he'd been on, the money he'd had to recover. He got a buzz out of it, and plenty of cash. 'There are so many opportunities out there,' he told me. 'We should do something when we get out.'

I lay in my cell for days, turning over the offer in my head. I was skint and had no idea what I wanted to do with the rest of my life. A lot of former Special Forces operatives go that way, and I couldn't blame them. With my training, I could easily and quickly become a very handy and respected asset within the top gangs in London. Whether it was surveillance, tracking people down, putting pressure on people, recovering debt or overseeing a job, it would be no problem. I was capable. I was aggressive. I could work with violence. The respect would automatically be there, there was plenty of money and it would come easy. The more I thought about it, the more it all added up. I could do it for a year, get some cash behind me and then move on. Why not?

After two months in Chelmsford I was transferred to Standford Hill prison on the Isle of Sheppey. It was an improvement, but I still didn't know when I'd be getting out. Of course, I hoped that I'd be released early for good behaviour, but there was no guarantee of that. And the pressure ratcheted up dramatically one day when I had a difficult call with Emilie. The moment she picked up the phone I could tell there was something wrong.

'It's money,' she said, when I finally got it out of her.

'You getting tight?'

'I'm really sorry, Ant, I've been trying my best. It's getting tricky. I've been doing the sums. If we don't start getting an income soon we're going to have to declare bankruptcy.'

'Bankruptcy?'

'Sorry, love. I've been looking for work that I can do in the evening when the kids ...'

'No, you don't,' I told her. 'You've got enough on your plate.'

'So what am I supposed to do?'

'I've got a parole interview this afternoon,' I told her. 'I can't promise anything. I'll do my best.'

I walked back to my cell ringing with shock and failure. I lay in bed for the next three hours, thinking, 'What an embarrassment. How shameful.' This was, without doubt, the worst thing about being inside. I'd become a burden on Emilie and my children. She'd even had to lie to the kids about me, telling them I was away with the military. I didn't belong in this place and I could never risk a return visit under any circumstances. And that meant resisting the gang life. It meant fighting that war of temptation in my head, and it meant fighting that instinct for violence that had been trained into me. I wasn't prepared to accept the excuses I heard again and again from former servicemen: 'Once a Marine, always a Marine' or 'I'm a soldier. I've been trained this way and you can't change me.' That was all rubbish. If I could train myself to be one of the most elite soldiers in the world, I could train myself to be one of the best civilians.

At 3.30 p.m. I turned up at the parole office, spick and span – and nervous. This would be the most important meeting of my life.

'I'm here for my interview,' I told the woman on reception.

'Name?'

'Middleton.'

She typed at her computer, barely even looking at me.

'You're cancelled. Come back next week.'

'Cancelled?' I said. 'That can't be right.'

'You need to return to your cell.'

'Why has it been cancelled?'

'You need to return to your cell immediately.'

'I'm just asking for a reason. When am I going to be seen?'

'Do I need to call a prison officer?'

I wanted to take a chair and launch it through the window. Instead, I made my way slowly back to the cells, breathing deeply, trying to hold it together. I was in prison for violence. One hint of aggression and any chance I had of parole would be blown.

As I turned the corner a young Scouser lad with a bowl haircut was coming the other way. He leaned in towards me as he passed, a hair's breadth from barging my shoulder.

'Fuck's sake,' I muttered.

He stopped. 'What's the matter with you?'

'Sorry, mate, I've just been told my parole interview's gone back a week,' I said. 'I just want to get out of here.'

He laughed in my face.

'Fuckin' hell, sort yerself out, la. Can't you even handle a little bit of bird? I've done more time inside than you've done on the shitter. You need to fuckin' man up, la, or you're going to get what's coming to ya.'

I could see the button in front of me. I could push it. I wanted so badly to push it. I just wanted to wipe the floor with him, smear him into the concrete, to belittle him, to let him know that he was nothing, that he was just a little gobshite.

'All right, mate,' I whispered.

I took a step back and watched him go on his way, with his cocky, bow-legged, shit-in-pants walk. If I'd had a couple more months to serve I'd have followed him into his cell and given him a shoeing. But I couldn't. The war wasn't with him, it was with myself. The effort it took not to knock him out was so immense I thought I might be having a stroke.

When my parole interview finally came it was one of the most nerve-wracking experiences I'd had. Behind the table, with their folders and pens, the parole officer, the prison chief and a social worker studied me with bored contempt.

'You're serving a term for a violent offence,' said the parole officer. 'What exactly have you changed about yourself?'

'I'm just keeping my positivity,' I said. 'There's a lot of pressure to push back in here, but I've been a model prisoner. The reason I've managed to do it is my family. They're waiting for me. I made a silly mistake due to alcohol. It was an error of judgement that ended up with me in this situation. I will never make that error again.'

'Right, Mr Middleton,' said the prison chief. 'Take a seat in the waiting area for ten minutes. We'll call you in when we're ready.'

Sitting in that room, with my right foot twitching, I counted every single movement of the clock's second hand. Finally, I was asked to come in and take my seat.

'On this occasion,' said the parole officer, unsmilingly, 'we have decided to allow you to serve the rest of your sentence at home, on a tag.'

For the next two days I hid in my cell. On my final morning I gave away everything I had, apart from the clothes I was wearing, to the other inmates – brand new trainers, brand new clothes, my radio, my books. I was determined that nothing to do with prison would contaminate my home life. I was escorted outside the gates to a guard room, where I was processed. The form-filling was endless. Then they had to go through the process of removing me from all their databases – getting signatures from the gym to take me off that database, then signatures from the health centre to take me off that database. It almost felt like a final test, just to see if I would snap.

After more than two hours I gave them my final signature. I had money left over from my canteen funds and they handed me £28.50 in a little money bag, as if I were a child. The prison officer arrived, shook my hand and wished me good luck. Then he opened a door and I simply walked out into the street. It was an ordinary day in the ordinary world and, just like that, I was in it.

Someone in a vehicle sounded their horn. On the other side of the road there was a small parking zone. Sitting in the family car was Emilie. I waited for a gap in the traffic and then ran across. I jumped into the passenger seat and she flung her arms around me.

'Don't ever do anything like that again,' she said. 'Promise me. No more fighting. I need you, Ant. *We* need you.'

I squeezed her tighter and felt her body soften.

'In your arms is my safe place,' she whispered, close to tears. 'It feels like home.'

'You are home,' I said. 'This a new beginning.'

I pulled away and looked deep into her beautiful green-brown eyes.

'This is where my life begins.'

LEADERSHIP LESSONS

The war is always in your head. You can't trust your body. It tells you it's got nothing left when it's still a hundred miles from breaking. And when it does actually break, it heals. The only true war you'll ever fight is with your own mind.

Be aware that situations can completely transform in an instant. On that night in Chelmsford I thought I was being the good guy, helping prevent a silly situation turning ugly. I was so caught up in my role as the hero, it simply hadn't occurred to me that I would end up being the villain. That transformation took seconds.

If it feels like 'temptation', it's a bad decision. It's easy to spot when a negative has presented itself to you – because you find yourself using the 'T' word. If you're tempted, as I was in prison, resist. You will rarely regret it.

Don't knock police officers out. Obviously.

THE POWER OF
INTELLIGENT WAITING

AFTER MY RELEASE from prison, the lure of instant respect and easy riches as part of a criminal firm wasn't the only temptation I had to resist. One day a representative from an African government asked me to take out the leader of the opposition, a gig for which I'd probably have been paid around £100,000. It would have been a pretty straightforward job, given that I'd have had the support of the government in question, but I didn't need to think about it for long. I'm not an assassin.

Although more conventional private security work soon started coming in, I did still receive the occasional unusual and intriguing offer. In March 2013 I took a call from a well-connected associate, a former Marine named Iain. My instructions were to be at a Middle Eastern restaurant on the Old Brompton Road at 11 a.m. sharp. The staff were just opening up when I arrived to find Iain already waiting at an outside table, along with a dark-haired guy in an expensive-looking camel-hair coat.

'Good to meet you, I'm Ant,' I said to the stranger.

He replied in an accent that was a mix of well-spoken English and Arabic. He was perhaps Saudi Arabian or Iraqi. 'Thank you for coming. I've heard some good things about you.'

'Good to know,' I said. 'Who from?'

'People,' he smiled. 'Please. Sit down.'

'Thanks,' I said, noting that he hadn't actually told me his name.

After the waiter had arrived with a plate of sweet pastries and an elaborate silver pot, from which he poured us each a strong black coffee into a glass cup, the man opened a leather satchel and took out an A4 envelope.

'I work as a correspondent for a certain family, organising this and that,' he explained vaguely. 'I have a job that I need carrying out expertly, discreetly and with the kind of *efficiency*' – he paused and looked at me and then Iain as he said the word – 'that men of your calibre and experience specialise in.'

'Go on,' I said, shuffling forward in my seat.

The correspondent pulled a small sheaf of documents from the envelope. His fingernails were perfectly manicured, the backs of his hands appeared waxed and, around his wrist, he wore a thin, bejewelled bracelet.

'I would like you to secure the release of this girl, Khalida Gulbuddin.'

He showed me a school photo. The girl looked mixed-race, with dark bobbed hair and large hazelnut eyes. She was smiling happily and openly at the camera.

'Someone's got her?' I said, pulling the picture towards me. 'Where is she?'

'To the best of our knowledge she's currently in Jordan. Her father is a powerful man, from Jordan himself, and has recently divorced my employer, Khalida's mother. There was a court case here in London. Custody was awarded to the mother. Unfortunately, shortly following the verdict, the father, whose name is Abdul Gulbuddin, took Khalida on a holiday to Jordan to visit relatives and failed to return. He has been gone for five months. In that time we have received no contact from him or anyone else in Abdul's extended family. My employer has now run out of patience.'

'I take it the local police ain't doing nothing?' asked Iain.

'Well, just as I said, Gulbuddin is powerful, wealthy.'

The correspondent moved his head left and right, as if weighing something up.

'And, more than that, it is also a cultural issue. In that part of the world a man's wants and wills always take precedence over a woman's. If the man wants the child, the man gets the child. If the woman cries about it, then so what? She is only a woman.'

I flicked through the court documents. 'And this is all we have to go on?'

'It is not much,' he admitted. 'But we do have one more thing.'

He took the papers from my hand and turned them over. On the back, written in navy blue ink from a fountain pen, was a Middle Eastern name and a string of numbers.

'This is the phone number of a friend who works for the Mukhabarat,' he said, pointing to one of them.

'What's that?' asked Iain.

'Jordan's security service,' he said.

'I know them,' I said. 'One of the best in the world.'

'That's right,' the correspondent nodded. 'Our friend is high up. She might be able to help you with some local information.'

'Good,' I said. 'Well, I feel confident we can get a result for you.'

I glanced at Iain. He didn't look like he was confident at all. But then neither was I.

'I hope that you can find Khalida,' he said. 'Please take my word for it, my employer is profoundly distressed by all that has happened. As a father yourself, I'm sure you can imagine. She needs you to succeed, very desperately. You are her final hope.'

As soon as I got home I called the number the correspondent had given us for the agent at the Mukhabarat. At first she was apologetic.

'I'm sorry, I can't help you with this,' she said. 'At least not actively.'

'What about contacts?' I asked. 'Addresses? Ideas of where she might be?'

'I can give you a couple of addresses, yes. Gulbuddin's father and his brother.'

'That would be a great start.'

'And if you can't persuade them to give the girl up, or at least tell you Abdul's whereabouts, I also have something else. The personal cell phone number of Nagid Hajjar, the head of Jordan's Public Security Directorate – the national police.'

'His cell phone?'

'Exactly,' she said. 'He will not know where or how you got this number. It will be a signal to him, if you call him on it, that you are connected. But please, don't tell him it was from us.'

THREE DAYS LATER, Iain and I pulled up in a taxi outside a large white house in a dusty suburb. The sun was pale yellow, the sky was pale yellow and the streets were covered in a layer of pale yellow sand. We were a short drive out of the twisted, choked and manic ancient centre of Amman, Jordan's capital, where we'd landed hours earlier. Iain paid the driver, who glanced back at us silently and nervously. I wasn't surprised he was uncomfortable. In his rear-view mirror I glimpsed our reflection. We'd deliberately gone for the thuggish look: sleeves rolled up, hair gelled back, muscles protruding. As I waited for all six foot five of Iain to unfold itself out of the cab, I felt a narrow trail of sweat slowly finding its way over the tattoo on my neck of the Grim Reaper with a glinting sickle. We'd need some luck, discipline and rigorous planning to pull this off, but I was determined we'd get Khalida back for her poor mother.

The gates of Gulbuddin's father's house were twelve feet high, heavy and black, with gold initials worked into the ironwork. They were also unlocked. The building behind them was surprisingly modest, two storeys high with a flat roof. There was a white Toyota Hilux parked outside the garage and a security light flicked on as we approached, despite the fact it was still early in the afternoon. A single dove perched on a grubby window sill, eyeing us coolly.

Iain knocked loudly, ignoring the bell. Our luck was in. Within seconds the old man appeared, grey bearded, hawk-nosed and visibly shocked – it was obvious from our appearance we weren't selling Girl Scout cookies.

'Mr Gulbuddin?' I asked.

'Who are you?'

'We're looking for your granddaughter, Khalida,' I said. 'She belongs back in the UK. We've been sent to fetch her home.'

'And what are your names?' he said. 'Who sent you? What is your right to come here, knocking on my door?'

'That doesn't matter. We're an independent investigation team.'

I gave him a piece of paper on which I'd written the number of the pay as you go mobile I'd bought downtown.

'I want to reassure you that our main interest isn't you, it's the girl. We need to get her back with her mother, as per the court's wishes.'

'I don't know where that girl is,' he said. 'I have not seen her for two years.'

Iain took a half a step forward. The old man pulled back into the shadows. Just as he was about to close the door, I shot my arm out and held it in place with my open hand.

'Mr Gulbuddin, we know that isn't true,' I said. 'So why don't you have a think about it? Please call me. If you don't, we will be back. We're not leaving this country until we find her.'

'Well, that went shit,' said Iain, back at the hotel.

He'd followed me into my room for a debrief and was sitting on the edge of my bed.

'What do you mean?' I said. 'You didn't think he was just going to scoop her up out of her crib and hand her over, all wrapped in swaddling clothes?'

'I didn't think we'd be knocking on doors and asking politely,' he said. 'That's not why we've been hired. We're not little old ladies. They want force. Pressure.'

'This isn't some smash-and-grab raid,' I said. 'We can't go in all guns blazing. We've got to wait.'

'Wait?' he muttered. 'Like old ladies at the bus stop.'

'You don't get it,' I said. 'Waiting is our best strategy right now. Waiting *is* force. Waiting *is* pressure. Waiting is a weapon.'

As frustrated as I was with Iain, I could also sympathise. The younger me would have simply smashed the fuck out of the grandfather, the grandmother and then the uncle. I'd have left them with no teeth and had them writing the address of Khalida's father across their kitchen tiles in blood.

But then what would have happened? We'd have been arrested and tortured, and then we'd have vanished. They'd have found us, weeks later, in some ditch with a bullet in the backs of our heads. We didn't have the cover of the armed forces behind us now, no flag of protection. There'd be no helicopter support for us, no airlifts out of tricky situations. We were on our own, in a stranger's land, and that meant playing a smarter game.

I knew that if this mission was going to work, it would have to be a psychological one. It was about planting the seed and waiting for it to grow. We'd planted it now. That was why I'd wanted us to arrive with our thug faces forwards. The moment we left the old man's house he'd have been straight on the phone to other members of the family. The fear and paranoia would already be spreading and growing, and the longer we allowed it to thicken and stretch, the greater its effect would be.

The power of intelligent waiting is something that's hugely underappreciated in the wider world. When you want to get a result it's human nature to want to steam in, to create action, to just get shit done. This is especially true for highly motivated, ambitious people. For them, waiting can feel too much like doing nothing. They begin to doubt themselves. The voice in their head says they're simply being lazy or, even worse, being weak – and that 'waiting' is just an excuse for doing nothing.

As long as you're doing it intelligently, this simply isn't true. In order to make waiting work as a strategy, you need two things: a plan, and strength of character. If you've made a smart plan with a series of execution points that you need to methodically hit, and waiting is a tactical part of that plan, then you're on. But having the spine to actually do it is just as crucial. You need to resist the voice that's telling you you're doing nothing, and the urge to pile in prematurely and force the issue.

It took me many years to learn this, and what impressed it upon me more than anything was my experience as a sniper. That lesson began with the first question my tutor asked of his rookie class of twenty or so, back at Lympstone Commando.

'When you hear the word "sniper", what do you think?'

He went around the room, asking random lads, and the answers came quick and predictable: 'One shot, one kill'; 'Headshot'; 'Thousand-metre shot'; 'Killing from a distance.' It was obvious from his expression that this was exactly what he was expecting to hear, and that we were wrong.

'Wind speed,' he said. 'Elevation. Breathing. Positioning. Camouflage. Humidity. Barometric pressure. The rotation of the earth. And, most importantly, patience.'

Training as a sniper was a revelation to me. It is the clos-est that soldiering gets to a fine art. In order to shoot accu-rately over distances measured in kilometres, everything has to be perfect. Every calculation you make has to be complete and correct. It involves a huge amount of planning, prepa-ration and brain power. And then it involves lots of waiting, often in the heat, wet or cold, sometimes for days. You need to have the patience to wait for the optimal moment and not go to the trigger a fraction of an instant before. Only once you've got all of that down can you take the shot. In a strange way, our mission in Jordan would also be a sniping game. It would be about careful planning and deadly patience.

The next two weeks were spent in our hotel rooms, wait-ing for the phone to ring. When it didn't, and Iain could no longer be reasonably contained, I agreed that we'd pay the girl's uncle a visit. His home turned out to be a huge ranch, an hour out of Amman. Despite the desert environment, he had luxurious lawns, serviced by sprinklers, on which were planted rows of perfect and massive palm trees, each heavy with coconuts. We drove our hire car slowly up the gravel drive and climbed the three steps up to the oversized front door.

After I'd pulled a steel handle to ring the bell, a Bangladeshi housekeeper answered, then went to fetch his master. Gulbuddin's brother soon appeared, in a traditional dish-dash and red plastic flip-flops. He wore little round Gandhi glasses and had a thin, drawn face, but there was just something about him. Despite his diminutive size, I sensed this was a man who wasn't easily intimidated.

'I hope you can help,' I said. 'We're an independent investigations team and we're looking for your brother.'

'My brother?' he said. 'I have three.'

'Abdul,' I said. 'It's Abdul that we want.'

'I haven't seen Abdul for years,' he said. 'Who are you, please? What is your business with Abdul?'

'Bullshit,' said Iain. 'You know exactly where he is and exactly what we want.'

I reached into my back pocket and pulled out a colour photocopy I'd made of Khalida's picture.

'You see this girl here? This is who we're after. If we do not find this girl, we're going to go through the whole of your fucking farm, every single floorboard, until we fucking find her. If you don't tell me where she is, we will turn this place upside down. Here are my contact details. Give me a call.'

When we returned, two days later, the ranch looked abandoned. The shutters were down. The door was bolted. The car was gone. They had fled.

'Great,' said Iain, glumly. 'Now what?'

'No, this is a good sign,' I told him. 'They're shitting it. It's working.'

Now that the fear was sinking in, it was time to add pressure from another direction. This next part of the plan would be a whole lot riskier. But as things stood, we had little choice. As Iain sat in a café on the corner of the bazaar, I stepped out into the street to place the call that could make or literally break us: the head of the feared Public Security Directorate.

'Is this Mr Hajjar?' I said to the voice who answered.

'Who is this?'

'My name is Daniel.'

'Daniel what?' he said. 'Who is this? How did you get this number?'

'What I can tell you is that I'm an independent investigation agent and I've come to recover a kidnapped girl who is being kept in your country.'

There was a silence.

'I know who you are,' he said, eventually. 'You have been making your presence felt in the city.'

'We are not leaving Jordan until we have the girl Khalida,' I replied. 'The courts have awarded custody to her mother. We have been sent to enact this verdict. If you guys aren't going to do anything to help this kidnapped girl, then I will make sure the international press are told the whole story, including your part in it. We will embarrass your country. We will embarrass you. We will let everyone know that we've had to come over here and do your job for you.'

With Hajjar promising to look into the case, I ended the call. It was another two days before the phone rang again.

'This is Nagid Hajjar. Would you be available to come in for a meeting?'

'When?'

'Let's say two hours. Noon. At the Public Security Directorate headquarters.'

This was a dangerous situation. We were strangers causing trouble in a nation not known for its adherence to human rights or legal niceties. Worse than that, we'd threatened the head of the dreaded Public Security Directorate. We'd made it personal. And now we were being beckoned into the belly of the whale. Hajjar had given us an address to go to, but what was actually at that address? Was it his office, or was it some kind of black site? We could easily be walking into a trap. As soon as I was off the phone, I called our contact at the Mukhabarat.

'Well, the address is correct,' she said. 'That is where Hajjar's office is.'

'Good,' I said.

'But that doesn't necessarily mean you're safe. Bad things happen in police cells in Jordan. Sometimes people don't leave them. You can only hope that your calling him on his cell has sent the right signal.' This wasn't the reassurance I'd been hoping for. But what else could we do?

* * *

251

IT WAS WHEN they started checking the individual hairs in my beard that I started getting nervous. 'These guys are offended,' I thought. 'We've really pissed them off.' We were standing in a back room being closely searched by two nameless goons in green military uniforms.

'What are you carrying?' they'd barked at us. 'Weapons? Recording devices?'

They took our phones away, removed the batteries, had the insoles out of our shoes and our socks turned inside out. They ran their hands up and down our bodies, their sweaty fingertips feeling all the way around the insides of our collars. Finding nothing of interest, we were led down a rickety spiral staircase into the basement. In front of us was a narrow corridor, its floor tiles chipped and polished, the grouting in between them brown with grime. The ceiling above us had a dark crack running down it. On either side of us, rows and rows of cell doors. Immediately, I started weighing options for what to do next. I had to admit what options we had were limited. These guys had pistols and billy-clubs. We were carrying only rage, dread and fists.

Just as I was about to act, we reached the end of a corridor, and a door made not of prison iron but of fake veneer wood. One of the goons knocked. We were shown into an office. It was neat and smart, with filing cabinets, a small barred window, a detailed and worn paper map of the city and, on the wall in the middle of the room, the requisite framed photograph of King Abdullah II. Sitting among it all was a man in his late fifties, stubbing out a cigarette, with a moustache, grey-black stubble and an immaculate uniform. On his desk was a tea pot, three small mugs and a silver bowl full of white sugar lumps. He was an obviously well-respected individual, but this office had an eeriness about it. If you ever found yourself here, you were in the shit.

'Thank you for coming at such short notice,' said Hajjar, indicating that we should sit. As we pulled out the chairs, his eyes drifted over our tattooed arms. I'd hoped we were sending the message that we were capable individuals who were choosing to go down a diplomatic route, for now – but that we were not going home with our hands in our pockets.

'I understand you are looking for a girl. How can we help you with this?'

I felt a surge of irritation at his now pretending he didn't know what we were here for. I felt Iain, beside me, bristle. From the back of my jeans I took out the folded court documents. Hajjar began pouring tea.

'We're independent investigators who are here to enforce the judgement of the British courts,' I said.

As I was talking be began pouring tea for me and Iain. I pushed the cups back towards him. There was every chance that if we drank it, we'd find ourselves waking up chained to a radiator.

'Please, you must be thirsty,' said Hajjar, pressing the point.

'I'll have a water. Bottled.'

Hajjar stood with a sigh and fetched two small bottles from a white mini-fridge in the corner. I made sure the seals opened with a crack before taking a swig.

'Well, before I can assist you,' Hajjar said, 'I first need some information from you, Mr Daniel. Who sent you? Who are you working for? Is it the girl's mother?'

'Not the mother,' I said. 'Someone else.' I lifted up the court documents. 'Khalida Gulbuddin belongs in the UK. She's a UK citizen. These court papers say so.'

'Yes, yes, yes,' he said. 'We're working very hard on this. Please, you must be assured that we have all hands on the case. A big team. This is being taken care of. A priority.'

'Reassurance isn't good enough,' growled Iain.

'Mr Hajjar,' I said, leaning forwards, my elbows on his desk. 'We're here to help. We're highly trained individuals and can be extremely useful to you. We want to be on your team, as members. We want to pitch in and assist you. I know exactly what needs to be done and I want to make sure that this is, as you say, a top priority. We aren't going to leave this country until the girl is on a flight home. If you let us pitch in, we can get this solved quickly and be out of your hair.'

'This is impossible, Mr Daniel. I don't even know who you are. Two big Englishmen, hunting for a beautiful young girl in my country. You could be anyone, with any purpose. I have a responsibility for this girl. I must ensure her safety.'

'When we find Khalida, we aren't expecting you to hand her to us,' I said. 'We expect the mother to fly to Jordan and collect her.'

He sat back and stewed for a moment.

'You can't be on the team,' he said. 'You definitely cannot.'

'So all you have to offer us is promises, promises?' said Iain. 'It's not fucking good enough.'

'I ask you for one week. We will prove our seriousness to you.'

'How?' I said.

'Just give me one week and I will contact you. What is your hotel?'

'You can call me when you have news,' I said. 'You've got my number. It's the one I phoned you on.'

Hajjar gnawed at the inside of his cheek, his eyes darkening.

'I am trying to help you, Mr Daniel,' he said, his voice low and menacing. 'But you sit in my office and you duck and you dodge and you treat *me* as if *I* am a criminal.' He sat still for a moment. 'It is you, Mr Daniel, who has entered my country, no doubt dishonestly on a tourist visa, and is travelling up and down making threats to citizens of Jordan.'

'Mr Hajjar ...'

'What hotel are you staying at?' he shouted.

'It's the ...'

I glanced at Iain. He looked away. I fumbled in my pocket, pulled out my key card and read from it.

'The Kempinski.' I looked up at him. 'There's only one Kempinski in the city, right? The one near the Bird Garden.'

'In Abdul Hamid Shouman Street,' he nodded, his eyes flicking down to the card for himself, presumably to check I wasn't lying. 'It's a wonderful place,' he said, happy now. 'Very fine breakfast at The Kempinski.'

'You have my number,' I said. 'If you're not happy with something, make sure you call me. Please be reassured that we're on your side. But, Mr Hajjar, you should also understand that if we have to take things into our own hands, we will.'

'We will be in touch with good news very soon, Mr Daniel,' he said. 'One week. Less.'

We were led out of the police station by the goons, hailed a cab and instructed it to take us to The Kempinski. Five minutes later, we ordered him to change course for the bazaar. We suspected they'd be trailing us and, sure enough, moments after we'd paid the driver and emerged onto the street, we became aware that we were being followed. Of course, what Hajjar and his men didn't know was that we were counter-surveillance trained and so we soon shook them off.

Once clear, we picked up some Turkish delight to nibble on and headed back up to The Kempinski. It was the best hotel in town and checking in there was the first thing we did on arrival in Jordan. But Hajjar was unaware that we'd checked out ten minutes later, told the receptionist the key cards were still in the room, pocketed them, then found a little backstreet place to use as a base. I'd anticipated the whole game, with the keycard at the police station, and it had worked like a dream. And, just as we suspected, they had people watching the hotel. We whiled away a pleasant afternoon in a cafe about two hundred metres away, eating baklava while surveilling our surveillance.

But despite Hajjar's promises, a week later we'd still heard nothing. I called him at noon, seven days to the minute following our meeting.

'Mr Daniel, we thought you'd left the country,' he said, clearly surprised we'd managed to entirely evade his team.

'You said a week,' I said. 'Nothing has happened. So we're going to come to your office and insert ourselves as part of the investigation team. We'll see you in forty-five minutes.'

'We're still working hard,' he said. 'But we need two more days. Just two more.'

'I'll give you three,' I said. 'But I'm worried. You tell me a week and I hear nothing, and I have to call you for news. Something's telling me you're not taking this seriously and the job isn't being done. But I'm personally taking this very seriously. I'm letting you know that if there isn't some good news in three days, we're taking things into our own hands. We're visiting families.'

'You have made the family very scared,' he said.

'I don't want to scare anyone, but I have a job to do.'

'Stay away from them, Mr Daniel. We can arrest you for this.'

'Three days. I am taking you on your word.'

Iain was not happy that we had yet more waiting to do. But this time it paid off. Three days later, Hajjar called to say that they had the girl. He refused to let us anywhere near her, insisting that his team hand her over to her mother, who had to fly in. The official reason was safety concerns for the girl, but I suspected it was about saving face. They wanted it to look like they'd done all the work, and deny our existence. That was fine by me. What wasn't fine, and what I didn't find out until we were back in the UK and Khalida's mother phoned to express her thanks, was that she'd been taken into a building at the perimeter of the airport and slapped about.

'But it's OK,' she said. 'I'm here. I'm alive. I have my daughter. Speaking honestly, I didn't think you'd get anywhere, apart from maybe in serious difficulty. Do you mind my asking, how did you do it?'

'How did we do it?' I said. 'Would you believe me if I said it was mostly a case of waiting?'

'No,' she laughed. 'I wouldn't believe it for a moment.'

LEADERSHIP LESSONS

Waiting is a weapon. It's human nature to want to steam straight in, especially for highly motivated people. It takes a stronger, smarter person to have the courage to wait. If it's done as part of an overall plan, waiting can be a deadly and vastly underappreciated tool.

Shame hurts. By threatening to expose Hajjar to the world as a corrupt or, even worse, an incompetent operator, I squeezed directly on the thing that was most important to him – his reputation. This applies to most people, especially if they're in any sort of position of power. If you publicly shame someone, you rip out their spine, their heart and their balls. That's a hurt that's often greater than any physical pain.

Wins are rarely clean. Life is complex, people are dangerous, and real fights usually cause damage to both sides. I was furious when I discovered that Khalida's mother had been assaulted, but I also knew that there was nothing I could have done about it.

HOW TO AVOID
A MUTINY

I WAS IRRITATED. But slightly amused. Rob Coldstream, a powerful commissioning editor at Channel 4, had invited me into his office to talk about a major TV project.

'It's an idea that's been bouncing around for a while, really, but we've just not found the right team to do it,' he said. 'It's for a show based on the Mutiny on the *Bounty*. It's tough. The idea is to recreate it. An epic sea voyage in a small sailing boat. Four thousand miles across the open Pacific, something like that, with someone taking the part of Captain Bligh and a bunch of lads along for the ride. After your success on *SAS*, we thought about you potentially taking the helm on it. Being Bligh.'

He put his pen down and narrowed his eyes.

'We've seen that you can talk the talk. Now let's see if you can walk the walk.'

I couldn't believe what he'd just said. Was he questioning my ability? Did he think I was just some Mouth Almighty? He wanted me to walk the fucking walk, did he? Had I not proved myself already? In that moment, in that airless corporate box in Central London, with its posters of daytime celebrities and cabinets filled with plastic awards, I felt the hatred poor out of me.

'Ha!' I laughed coldly, looking straight back at him. 'Ha! OK. I see what you're saying.'

'What do you think, then?' he said. 'Could you handle it?'

'Oh, I'll deliver on this, don't you worry about that.'

'I hope so.' He studied my face doubtfully. 'I will remember this conversation.'

Before I'd even made it to the revolving doors of Channel 4's headquarters, I'd flipped the bad feeling that had flooded me. That anger became fuel – the negative became positive; my enemy became my energy. 'I'll show him,' I thought. 'I'll smash it. I've got to get this right.' The only problem was, I didn't exactly know what I'd promised to deliver on. *The Mutiny on the Bounty*? Wasn't that some old-school Hollywood pirate movie? And who was Captain Bligh anyway?

'He was the captain of a ship, same age as you. Kicked off his boat in 1789 in the South Pacific,' explained David Dugan, the founder of Windfall Films, the company that had been tasked by Channel 4 to actually make the show. We'd met for lunch and he was filling in the gaps for me. 'Bligh and his men were left for dead in a tiny rescue boat.'

'Tiny?' I asked.

'Twenty-three foot,' he said.

'Tiny,' I nodded.

'You've had plenty of experience on the sea, is that right?'

'I've always loved the ocean. It's the challenge of it. The unknown and the danger.'

'And in the military?'

'I served on HMS *Ocean* before I was deployed to Afghanistan. I'm an able seaman.'

'Well, that's great. You'll be leading a band of men, just like it was back in 1789. We want to keep it as authentic as possible.'

As he said the word 'authentic' my ears pricked up.

'We plan on building an exact replica of the boat. It's all open, so you'll be exposed to all the elements.'

'That's exactly how I'd want to do it too,' I said. 'What did they eat back then?'

'They were on ship's biscuits and salted pork. About 380 calories a day.'

'We need to be on 380 calories a day then. How do you make ship's biscuits?'

'Flour, salt and a bit of water?'

'Well, we'll need to get those made up. What about the salted pork?'

'That's going to be harder to source.'

'We could use biltong. It's exactly the same. How much of it did they have?

'Thirty-three grams a day.'

'Then that's what we'll eat: 380 calories, ship's biscuits, biltong.'

A shadow of doubt flashed across David's face. I carried on regardless.

'What did they wear?'

'Cotton, canvas and silk.'

'Nothing can be waterproof. We need to feel the elements like they felt them.'

'We'll have to see. It might be a bit of a problem getting that past health and safety.'

I sat back in my chair, resting my elbow on the clean white tablecloth.

'David, if you're going to have everything authentic all the way down, you can't do the journey in fucking waterproof clothes. That defeats the object.'

By now he was looking gravely concerned.

'Well, we'll have to look into it,' he said. 'Check the legality. You have to understand, though, you will need *some* modern accoutrements. Like GPS.'

'We can't have GPS on board!' I cried. 'We need to use a sextant and old paper charts, just like they did. There's no point otherwise.'

He clearly thought I was mad.

Over the next few weeks, as more details about their plans emerged, I became increasingly excited. They wanted to mirror the people that were on the original boat as closely as possible. Bligh was a young military leader, I was a young military leader. He had sailing masters on board and we would too – Conrad, an old boy who'd sailed around the world; young Freddy, who'd sailed the Cape; and Chris, who'd sailed around the UK. Bligh had a medic on board and we'd have a junior GP called Luke. Bligh had a carpenter and we'd have handyman Ben. There was also a City boy called Rish on our crew, who made a living selling expensive whisky to high-end pubs and clubs. I'm not really sure why he was there and, by his own slightly baffled admission, neither was he. Anyway, he'd be our quartermaster, dishing out food and water.

The combined forces of health and safety and insurance dictated that we'd only have half the number of men that Bligh had. It also meant that, despite my protestations, we'd have to keep a GPS on the boat, if only to be used in emergencies. But I fought back as much as I could, on every little detail. For me, if it wasn't essentially true to Bligh's actual experience, it wasn't worth doing. I was determined that the crew and I had to exist within a bubble of authenticity, and that this bubble would not be broken. I understood that they wanted to track us in a safety boat, but I insisted that it had to stay over the horizon at all times, where we couldn't see or hear it. We'd need to feel that we, as a team, had only one option: to get ourselves out of the shit. It's impossible to get into that mindset if you can just glance over your shoulder and see the promise of warmth, safety and a supply of Rich Tea biscuits.

The first time I met the men who I'd be captaining was for a group briefing and medical examinations at the Union

Jack Club in Waterloo. This was yet more insurance and health and safety business, including a full health MOT, and blood tests for liver function, hepatitis B and C, and HIV. Then, more painful than a million blood tests, was a health and safety briefing that we had to attend to satisfy the insurance company. Sitting politely around a long table in a boardroom, somewhere deep in the military club, we learned that there were sharks in the ocean, that sharks can be naughty, that it was possible to drown in water and that, when moving around the wooden boat, we should be careful of splinters.

I might have acted as if I was taking this entertainment show with heavy seriousness, but behind the scenes I'd spent the preceding weeks pushing for as little health and safety as possible. It was a whirlwind of argument, counter-argument and compromise. I eventually allowed life jackets, but they were only to be worn at my discretion. I also had to permit the use of clip-on harnesses for use in stormy seas. One big sticking point for me was the waterproofs. The production company were insistent, but I genuinely believed we didn't need them. I wanted to prove that a good leader can take any body of men or women and mould them into people who can get the job done.

But even more than that, I wanted to prove that modern-day man is every bit as tough as men used to be. There's an old saying that 'when ships were made of wood, men were made of steel.' When it's said today, what it's really implying is that, in the modern age, ships are made of steel and men of wood. I wanted to show the world that this isn't true. I'd take an average City boy and mould him into something gritty and hard.

I believe there's still a primal caveman instinct in all of us – a core of masculinity. Most men today are wrapped in cotton wool. Nobody is held responsible for their actions. Men aren't allowed to be men anymore. I wanted to take a bunch of lads and turn them into a formidable team. We were going to suffer together, have a fucking good time together and show the world that we were every bit as tough as those lads were in 1789. I was going to take this mission to the line and push it over.

But when the others heard about my plans they fell silent. Having delivered my impassioned speech, following the health and safety man's exit, I was met by awkward stares and shuffling. I excused myself to use the bathroom and, as soon as I was in the corridor, I heard the negativity start: 'I don't think he understands the open ocean'; 'He's being naïve'; 'He's being reckless'; 'There's doing it authentically and then there's being stupid.' When I returned I dug in, pressing the point even further.

'Don't get it into your heads that we'll be doing this by the book,' I said. 'Once we're on the sea, that book goes out of the window. We'll need to break the rules to survive.'

At this, Conrad piped up. He was the most experienced sailor in the room by far, but he'd done it all using ultramodern equipment, with the capability to shelter below decks for a nice cup of tea when the weather turned.

'No,' he said. 'I'm sorry, it just doesn't work like that.'

'Listen, I respect what you've done,' I replied. 'You've sailed around the world and I tip my hat to you. But get all this health and safety shit out of your head. Forget the idea that this is a sailing trip. This is not a sailing trip. This is one of the hardest and biggest survival feats in the history of mankind. This is about staying alive. You – all of you – need to get yourselves into that mindset.'

Conrad said nothing, but I could tell what he was thinking: that he was the experienced sailor, I was just some shouty guy from the telly who was only there to be a public figurehead. There was no way I was going to let him, or the group, define me like this. I decided that, for the time being, starting a head-to-head ruction with this guy would be the wrong strategy. Instead, I'd allow him to feel like the big man, while observing him, working out his strong points and weak spots. I'd quietly lead from behind. I'd sit back and let him stride about with his chin up. But when the time came, I'd earn his respect. The time would come when I'd show him exactly why I was captain, of that I had no doubt.

The other crew member I was worried about that day was handyman Ben. He was overweight, gobby and kept trying to be funny, snapping, 'Yes, Sergeant Major!' at me. I let him have his little games, while thinking that if we were in the military, I'd have ripped his fucking head off. His sarcasm, I knew, was going to wear thin very quickly. It also didn't speak well of his character. Here was a guy who wasn't very proactive and hid behind his humour. That was all well and good when you were living a mediocre existence in suburban London, but what was he going to do when he was in a world of pain in the middle of the ocean? What would he have to offer then, apart from some dim joke?

The others seemed fine. Rish the City boy was cheery and positive. Freddy was keen, had done his maritime qualifications, worked on cargo ships and super yachts, and even spent half his year living on his dad's boat. He was a sailing geek who could tell you the star formations and which way up to hold a sextant. He'd be a good member of the team, although he seemed fragile. Chris, meanwhile, was a birdlike Scouser who'd sailed solo around the UK. He was respectful, self-taught and seemed to know his stuff, but there was a rebellious edge to him. I could see myself a little bit in him. Out of everyone, I thought he'd be the greatest asset to the team. Then there were Sam and Dan, the embedded cameramen, who both had experience in the survival world. I was glad to have them onside, as they understood where I was coming from and why I'd been tapped to lead this mission. This would be a survival situation. It would be serious. I'd need to play every individual in this raggedy crew to their strengths. I wouldn't have time to develop weaknesses.

After the health and safety meeting everyone agreed to head off for beers so they could all bond. But I didn't want to hang around and mix with the crew. We weren't going on a holiday together. I wanted to keep a separation between us. Leaders stand apart from crowds, and I didn't want familiarity to get in the way of the respect I'd need to get the job done. I wasn't there to be their pal, I was there to be their leader. If I was getting stuck into the beers and playing stupid games with them one day, then having to lay down the law the next, their immediate, instinctive response would be, 'Who the fuck do you think you are?' That attitude could lead to festering and toxicity among the men. It might ultimately be the thing that would sink us.

Two weeks before they all arrived in Tonga, where we'd launch out into the mission, the production crew and I flew out to make final plans. The place was pure paradise – everything you're imagining right now, as you read this, was there. We stayed in a nice hotel along the beach, away from where the others would be put up. After they landed I restricted my time with them to a pizza and a couple of beers, before going back to my hotel. They were noticeably cautious around me. The magnitude of the task was finally hitting them, and I've no doubt that the general feeling among them was, 'Fucking hell, we have this guy off the telly who's not even a sailor leading us. How the hell is this going to work?'

Shortly before the morning of our departure I had another difficult exchange with Conrad. We were having dinner at the hotel, charting the route, when discussion fell to the crew's sleep and work patterns. He wanted to do it in three shifts, so three men were up at a time while six men slept.

'No,' I said. 'That's not going to work. We need four on and four off and I, as captain, will sit back jump between shifts so I can have an overall view of things.'

He pulled a face like he was passing something knotty.

'This is not the kind of boat you're used to, where everyone has their own bed,' I said. 'Because of the space, if we did 3–3–3, we'd have to hotbed around the boat.'

'But what's wrong with that?' he said. 'Explain.'

'I'll explain,' I said. 'It's going to be sheer hell out there. And, with the greatest respect, Conrad, I've been to hell. I've survived hell. I know what hell is like. It's critical for morale that the men are able to go back to what they think of as their own safe haven. I'm going to get people to pair up, so each pair has its regular spot. Then, when they change over, they return to their familiar bed space. I'll sleep anywhere on the boat, I don't mind. But I need those guys to know they have their cocoon to crawl back into. And I need them to slot into a routine. I want them sleeping where their stuff is, knowing where to find everything, so they can make every second count and get as much sleep as possible.'

He still looked ill at ease. 'Well, let's go with your plan to begin with,' he said. 'See how it goes.'

'We're going to need to maintain tight discipline,' I said. 'Tie everything down, make sure everything is put away. When a man gets into his bed space, if his partner's shit is everywhere, it's going to annoy him and grind on him and he's going to lose sleep because it will be ticking through his head. That mindset can eat away at you. We're not out there for two weeks. It's two months. We've got two sets of clothes each. Everyone has to make sure their dry set is packed away properly so it doesn't get wet. If waves come over, if shit hits the fan, at least you know you've got a nice dry set of kit to climb into when it's all over. The war out there, it won't be with the ocean. The war we'll be fighting will be in our own heads.'

'They're going to find all this a bit strict,' he said. 'It's all very military. They won't be used to it.'

'Yeah, but once people get into it they love that discipline. Trust me. They'll be so glad to be getting back to their familiar cocoon, not having to sort their partner's shit out, knowing exactly where their spoon and cup is. They'll learn to value the discipline very quickly. And if they don't, they won't make it.'

'OK,' he said cautiously. 'We can always juggle things about if your system doesn't work out.'

In between these planning meetings we were having regular capsize drills. I'd decided that we'd each have a number, and once we bobbed back to the surface we'd call our number out. That's how we'd know everyone was present and correct. During one of the first drills we were bobbing away and listening for the numbers: 'One!' 'Two!' 'Three!' ... No four. Who was number four? It was Dan the cameraman. All we could hear was the wind and the lapping of the sea knocking against the wood of the upturned hull.

'Where's Dan?' someone said.

'Ssssh!' I hissed. 'Shut up!'

There was a faint knocking. I knew immediately what had happened. Dan was trapped under the boat. Without thinking, I kicked into work mode, dived under and dragged him out. It was a scary situation, but an important moment for the development of the team. It was the first time I was able to show the men why I'd been selected to lead this mission.

Before we knew it, the day had arrived. We woke at 4 a.m. on the safety boat, which was dragging *Bounty's End* – our home for the next two months – behind it. We showered, were thoroughly searched for contraband, our bags emptied and checked, then we were all quarantined together until we reached the location where, more than two centuries ago, the mutineer Fletcher Christian had committed his treacherous act.

I looked out of the porthole at the weather. 'Look at the swell out there,' I said, to no one in particular. 'It's going to be rough.'

And then we were called forwards. We clambered down a ladder into *Bounty's End* and our white canvas duffel bags were literally thrown in after us. The mood on the boat was wild. Everyone was raring to go. It was great to see such energy, but I had to get their minds on the game.

'Listen, we're on our own now,' I told them from my place up at the tiller. 'Get that safety ship out of your heads. That's not fucking happening. It's just us. The only people who can get us out of this situation are ourselves, as a team. You can always choose to get back on that safety boat if you like. But if you do, you're not stepping foot back on *Bounty's End*. We have a job to do. Let's get those sails up.'

As the safety boat disappeared over the edge of our watery world, we began to feel as lost, tiny and vulnerable as a midge that had been fired into space. Our first task was to get into the nearest island, which was about a day away. I knew it was called Tofua and that this was obviously the location Bligh went to, but beyond that I didn't know much about the original voyage we were meant to be tracking. I deliberately didn't read up on Bligh himself or read his journal of the voyage, which was published as *The Mutiny on the Bounty*. I didn't want to poison my mind by thinking how someone else did it. I wanted to do it my way. I was charting his journey, but doing it as me. Besides, it was also about authenticity. Captain Bligh didn't have a book to guide him, and I didn't want one either.

That night, a terrible storm blew in. The wind picked up in the early evening and, by 7 o'clock we were miserable, wet-through and being tossed about like a leaf in the wind. And we were starving. Our ration was three ship's biscuits per day. Not only were they tasteless, they were so hard I broke a tooth on one of them. For our evening meal we'd be treated to thirty-three grams of biltong, which amounted to barely a mouthful. The dryness of the food wasn't helped by the lack of water, which we were rationed to a litre and a half a day each. Enough to survive but, in that heat, nowhere near enough to provide anything like comfort. Making the situation worse was the fact that people weren't sleeping when they should've been. As hard as they might try, they were finding it impossible. It was freezing, water was coming over the side of the boat and drenching them, and they were in a state of chronic shock.

The next day, the weather had stilled, and a beautiful morning dawned on the coast of Tofua. I'd decided that three of us would go onto land, while everyone else stayed on board, making sure the boat didn't crack up against the rocks. I took Chris with me and instructed him to find coconuts, while I tried to locate a water source to bolster our supplies, with Dan in tow, filming. Before I headed inland I found a little camp where we'd sleep the night, with good visuals of the boat around two hundred metres away.

'You can be the liaising point to the ship,' I said to Chris. 'Shout if you need me. But while you're here, I want you to collect firewood and make this campsite a bit more liveable, so we can have a half-comfortable sleep tonight.'

'Yeah fine, mate,' he said.

What I didn't realise, as I tracked into the bush, was that he'd taken this badly. For some reason he'd interpreted my perfectly standard request as treating him 'like a ten-year-old'. When Dan and I were safely out of the way, he started moaning, mucking about and jumping off the high, jagged rocks into the sea.

The boys in the boat were shouting at him, 'Get off the rocks! Stop jumping! You're going to injure yourself.'

His attitude was simply, 'Fuck off. I can do what I like.'

While all this was going on, Dan and I were enduring a tough and fruitless search for water, climbing the slopes of a volcanic island with the power of the midday South Pacific sun set to maximum. We had nothing to drink – all the liquids were still on the boat. We ended the day with nothing to show but serious dehydration and a bunch of coconuts.

The next morning we hauled the coconuts back onto *Bounty's End*. As soon as I was back on board, Conrad pulled me to one side.

'Why did you let Chris jump off the rocks?' he said.

'Was he?'

'Yeah, we were shouting at him not to be so stupid, but he took no notice.'

'Well, mate, I didn't know,' I said. 'I was up a volcano looking for water. But you know, Chris is all right. He was busy getting firewood. It's fine.'

I was a bit perturbed at what I was hearing, but my priority was to maintain team unity. Even though I'd stuck up for Chris, I knew I'd have to keep a close eye on his attitude. It was only day two, and already he'd knocked a crack into the precious relationship between me and the crew.

Our next leg – to Yadua Island – was going to be around five hundred miles, and a few days into it we found ourselves heading right into the centre of an epic storm. Conditions became so bad that if we'd run into life-threatening trouble, the safety boat wouldn't have been able to get us. They couldn't risk the lives of their crew by sending men out in a small boat, and if the main ship pulled up beside us, the waters were so fierce there'd be a serious risk of it smashing *Bounty's End* to pieces.

On and on it went, hour after hour, water pouring over the sides of the boat as if it wasn't us but the whole world that was being violently thrown about. It's no exaggeration to say that we weren't floating anymore – we were literally surfing the swells. The men were huddled in the hull, praying. During the night we lost communication with the safety ship.

'Guys, this is fucking serious now,' I said. 'If we flip, we're dead. I need everyone to be alert.'

As conditions grew worse still, I ordered Conrad to man the helm with me and instructed everyone to bed down where they could and keep as dry as possible, using material we kept to repair damage to the sails as cover. They didn't have to do any work. Their only job was to stay alive. Conrad and I would take care of the rest.

As morning dawned on the second day of the storm, nothing looked any better. The swell was still huge, and the men were wet, cold and shaking, just as you would be if you'd been soaking in a bathtub of freezing water for thirty-six hours. We'd been so relentlessly wet, for so long, that our fingers started to rot. It had come to feel as if the rain was hitting through our skulls and impacting our brains directly. Sam the cameraman, who'd been struggling valiantly to capture what he could of our situation, had chunks of skin sloughing off his fingers. Fred was shitting and vomiting at the same time and involving himself in the mad gymnastics of simultaneously trying to get both ends of his dribbling body facing out towards the sea. Meanwhile, Chris the sailor was so catatonic that Conrad and I had to undress him, rinse out his clothes and put them back on again for him. Even in the midst of all that misery and discomfort, the irony brought a smile to my face: he'd complained of being treated like a ten-year-old and now, because of his own lack of sea legs, we were being forced to treat him like a ten-*month*-old.

Finally, on day three, we exited the eye of the storm. It was scant relief. We still had the rest of the system to push through. We would, I guessed, be dealing with another two days of this. At some point that morning Ben shuffled over to me, with a face on him like an abused dog.

'Ant,' he said. 'I need to dry off. I really do. I need to get on the safety boat. Just to get dry. Then I'm back in.'

'That's not an option,' I told him. 'If you get on that boat, you're not coming back. That's it.'

He crawled back down to the other end of the boat and reported back what I'd said to the rest of them. Beneath the roar of the swell and the beating of the sails, my ears focused into their voices.

'We can't be treated like this,' said someone.

'Yeah,' said someone else. 'No one ever told us it would be like this.'

I couldn't let this continue for another second.

'Oi!' I shouted. 'That's enough of that fucking negativity. The only people who put you into this situation is yourselves. We're all volunteers here. Nobody's forced us on this boat. You have two options. You can get off this boat and know you're not coming back on it. Or we can all gather together as a team and fucking smash through this together. Before you know it, we'll be on the next island. You'll be able to rest up, get your kit dry and maybe even have some decent food.'

I was met with nothing but sorry silence from the crew. In the end, the storm raged, and the rain came down, for ninety-six straight hours.

By the time we landed on Yadua I felt my position as captain had finally been earned. I'd not slept. I'd kept the boat upright and sailing in the right direction. I'd got them through it, just as I'd promised. What's more, I'd come to respect Conrad, and he'd come to respect me. As my second-in-command, he'd truly stepped up.

With the relief of hitting dry, still land for a three-day stint, the stress lifted and the less attractive edges to some of the crew started to show. Ben, especially, was highlighting himself with his laziness, leaving his mess everywhere around the camp. When I pulled him up on it, he dismissed the rules I was trying to impose as 'just campfire games'. I tried to impress upon him that, aside from morale, it was important keep everything squared away in case anything went wrong. We needed to be able to grab all our kit and escape in a hurry if necessary.

I know a few of them were looking around at our situation, camping out on a paradise beach, and thinking, 'What exactly could go wrong in a place like this?' But twelve hours after our arrival a tsunami warning came over the emergency radio. We were in the middle of cooking a big crab stew and, because I'd insisted on camp discipline, we were all safely on high ground, crab stew and all, within minutes. When the threat had passed I took Ben aside for a quiet word.

'Look, I know you've got loads more in you. I need you to step up. I need more self-confidence. You need to stop hiding behind your humour because when that goes, you're a burden.'

The next leg was a big one. Two weeks and seven hundred miles lay between us and Vanuatu. But by the time we launched off, everyone was raring to go. If we'd survived that four-day storm, we could survive anything. Even Ben was bucking his ideas up. We hadn't been long back at sea, though, before Chris started to struggle getting out of bed in time for his shifts. First he was five minutes late, then ten minutes. His kit was everywhere. He was supposed to be helping with the navigation, using the sextant and charts, but he kept making mistakes. After a while I began to wonder whether he even knew how to use it but, when questioned, he'd insist that he did. Before long I found myself having to haul him up, and every time I did I'd be met with a variation on the same response, which was that either me – or everyone else – was treating him like a kid.

'We're not treating you like a kid,' I'd say. 'We're asking you to be a member of this crew. Do you need some help? If you don't understand something, that's all right, but you have to tell me. I'll help you.'

'I don't need any help. I'm not a ten-year-old. I've sailed round bloody Britain.'

If sleeping in and leaving his mess everywhere wasn't frustrating enough in that small space, he'd stopped washing. When it was calm, the rest of us would jump into the water and have a good scrub, but he refused. He stunk like a rotting badger. And the layer of dirt he was living beneath soon started to have knock-on effects. He cut his leg, somehow, and the wound became heavily infected. He was getting ulcers in his skin, including one in his armpit that burst open. Freddy, the young lad that was unfortunate enough to be sharing boat space with him, was livid.

One night he was on shift, navigating with the sextant while I was taking the opportunity to get my head down. By the time I woke up, the light was just starting to break into morning. As Chris crawled in bed, I inspected the charts to see the navigational marks he'd made on them. I couldn't see any there.

'Chris, mate?' I said. 'Have you taken the sextant reading? Where's the mark?'

'I didn't take a reading,' he said. 'Whoever left the sextant like that set it up wrong.'

This made exactly zero sense.

'What do you mean "set it up wrong"? When you pick up a sextant, you put all the settings back to normal.'

'Yeah, well, I didn't record our position because ...'

'Chris, do you know how to use it?'

''Course I fucking do.'

'Come up and show me then,' I demanded. 'Show me how to use it.'

As Conrad and Freddy looked on, he demonstrated quickly that he had no idea at all. 'How the fuck can you not know how to use it?' I said.

'You're treating me like a kid and belittling me,' he wailed. 'I'm sick of this.'

Because of Chris's fear of admitting any form of weakness, we'd sailed twenty miles off course. Nobody expected him to know how to sail an eighteenth-century boat. I'd have shown him in a heartbeat and that would've been that. But all that time he'd been dodging the truth and letting it grow in his head, and now it had come back at him. He'd allowed his mistake to win.

And because he had, the rest of the crew were deciding they'd finally had enough. The whispers went round the boat, as soft and seductive as the warm breeze that was lifting off the Pacific's crystalline surface: 'He's sleeping in again'; 'He stinks'; 'He's got a bad attitude'; 'He's isolating himself'; 'I want him gone.' One day he slept through three shifts straight. When he eventually did wake up he had the audacity to complain: 'Fucking hell, I've had no sleep.'

Things came to a head on Vanuatu. I'd never seen a place so perfect, and everyone was sensationally happy, on a high better than any drug. We fell in with some wonderful locals, ate from their gardens – replanting everything we'd picked – and went pig hunting with them. The only blot on the landscape was Chris. For some unknown reason he made the decision to go wild pig hunting with all his thermal underwear on. He was sweating and struggling and moaning, playing the victim as usual and slowing the rest of us down. We were embarrassed by him. As a leader I felt I was representing all of these lads in front of the Vanuatuans, who I'd come to think extremely highly of. He was shaming all of us. I just wanted him to disappear.

That night, I was grabbing a bit of kip in my hut when I was suddenly woken up. It was Conrad.

'The guys want to have a bit of a chat,' he told me 'It's about Chris.'

I rubbed my eyes and staggered onto the moonlit beach. I'd had a feeling this was coming. It turned out that Chris was sleeping, too, and the lads had taken the opportunity to let me know what was on their minds.

'Right, guys,' I said. 'If you've got an issue about Chris, you need to voice it.'

After a moment of quiet, Freddy spoke up.

'I know this sounds bad,' he said, 'but if I knew he was going to be on that boat for the rest of the trip and he was going to be the same, I don't think I'd do it, to be honest. He's driving everybody mad.'

'You want him off then?' I asked. 'Who else feels like this?'

'In the last few days I realise how little he does for the group,' said mild-mannered Luke. 'Essentially, we're carrying him. And it's pissing me off.'

After they'd all voiced their opinions, I went round, one by one, asking for a simple yes or no answer to the question, 'Do you want Chris on the boat with you?' Only Ben said yes. I promised I'd make a decision and inform them of it the next day. I tried to sleep but couldn't, and ended up staring into the dying flames of the fire for hours. What was I going to do? I'd put my head on the chopping block many times for Chris, and each time he'd let me down. But it was by no means a straightforward decision. Losing a man like this would be a failure, in my eyes. Yet feelings were running very high. It was turning out to be a test of my leadership. I'd somehow found myself teetering on the brink of a genuine mutiny.

First thing the next morning, I pulled Chris aside. Perched on a piece of fallen tree, I asked him to sit down next to me. I gave it to him straight.

'None of them want you on the boat.'

'I don't get it. What have I done wrong?'

'The lads don't think you're a team player, you're dangerous on the boat and you're a hindrance to the team.'

He shook his head in shock and confusion, as if I was telling him the moon was made out of cheese.

'That's just ridiculous.'

'They're saying to me, "Ant, why are you allowing him to get away with all this?"'

'I carried the water …' he interrupted me.

'Listen! Listen! Listen!'

But he kept talking.

'Fucking listen to me!' I shouted. 'Listen to what I've got to say. I'm trying to help you out, here, but you're talking over me. You're pissing me off.'

After we'd spoken, he promised to go away and think about it. But, predictably, he made his crewmates the issue and started having a pop at them for being 'two-faced' for coming to me. He had no conception whatsoever of how his own actions had contributed to the situation. As far as he was concerned, the only problem on *Bounty's End* was everyone else.

And unfortunately for Chris, his only ally on the team was running into his own problems. It soon came to light that, through fear of being kicked off the boat, Ben had been hiding a serious infection in his hand from a cut he'd sustained at some point during the previous sail. His hand was swollen like a cadaver's and the poison, hard and painful, was spreading up his arm.

The sadness of the situation was that Ben was just coming into his own. He was using his carpentry skills to help the locals build houses, and you could tell that this was an important, precious experience for him. He was inspired. Even the stupid jokes had almost stopped. When the decision was made that his hand was in a bad enough state to require urgent hospital treatment, he was devastated. We stood on the beach and watched him leave for the safety boat, and more than one of the lads were crying genuine tears. Perhaps they were sorry to see him go; perhaps they were upset that it wasn't Chris we were watching vanish into the endless blue.

But it wasn't. After his tantrum, Chris came to me, apologised and promised to drop the attitude.

'I'm a man down, now that Ben has gone,' I told him. 'I need you more than ever. I've got your back.'

As far as I was concerned, this was a line drawn under it. Chris had apologised. He had promised to sort himself out. He was in. But news of my decision was greeted by the others like a wet fart.

'Chris will be staying with us, full stop,' I told them. 'I can't go from nine men to seven men. I don't want to hear anything else about it.'

I understood their response, but it was essential – now more than ever – that we all united together as a team. The next leg of the journey was going to be a killer seventeen-day slog over 1,600 miles of open ocean.

We pointed the boat west, in the direction of Restoration Island, off the coast of Australia. As the wind filled both sails, I noticed with delight that Chris had turned himself around. His attitude was better, he was helpful and positive and getting out of bed. Watching him from my place at the tiller, I was glad I hadn't given up on him.

It didn't last. As the voyage grew arduous, and the twin vultures of hunger and boredom started eating us alive once more, he crumbled. He slept in and, when I ordered him to get up, he accused me once again of belittling him and treating him 'like a ten-year-old'. I didn't know where all this 'kid' stuff was coming from, and I had no interest in finding out. But what I knew for sure was that Chris seemed like a classic case of a man who had demons that he'd not made friends with. There seemed to be a deep and raging anger inside him that I guess was somehow connected to his paranoia about being viewed as a child. The tragedy was that, by embracing this darkness and making it an ally, he'd be able to access an almost limitless battery of energy. Forget Timor, where Bligh and his crew ended up, he could sail to the moon. But, as it was, these demons were taking his soul.

And, sure enough, carried on the hot ocean wind, I began hearing the whispers again; men threatening to leave because they couldn't deal with him. One afternoon, Luke asked to have a word with me in the stern, which was the only place on *Bounty's End* where anyone could have anything like a private conversation.

'Can I ask you something?' he said carefully. 'Why are you concentrating all your energy on something that's not working?'

'What do you mean?'

'You've given him so many chances and put your head on the chopping block for him so many times. Why are you neglecting us, the rest of the crew?'

'Do you really feel like that?' I said. 'That I'm neglecting you lot?'

'Yes, of course,' he said. 'We'd love a bit of the time and energy you're putting into him.'

That was it. He had to go. And I knew exactly how to manipulate him into walking himself off that gangplank. The next time he overslept, I aimed at little speech right at the centre of that brittle little heart of his.

'You're nothing but a fucking burden,' I told him. 'Who put you on your high horse and told you you're a good sailor? You're not. You haven't got a fucking clue. You're a liability. It's like looking after a child, a fucking baby. We're all nursing you. From now on, do what you want. Just keep yourself out of our way. You can be a passenger aboard our vessel. We will get you to the end, but when you get there, know this: it hasn't been you, it's been us.'

He reacted exactly as I expected him to.

'I don't deserve this,' he said. 'I want off the boat.'

After giving a sheepish interview to the camera, he was picked up by a launch from the safety boat. We watched that dark element depart with pure joy in our souls. The next time I'd see his face would be staring out of a tabloid newspaper: he'd been handed a suspended sentence for harassing an ex-girlfriend and threatening to throw acid in her face. In a single day he called her fifty-seven times, from nine different numbers. He even went to her house and shouted through her letterbox. And guess what he shouted? 'I don't deserve this.'

The next two weeks passed in a daze. By now the arduousness of the voyage and the lack of food and water were truly taking their toll. All of us, including me, were sitting on the bones of our arses. Back at Vanuatu we'd felt as if we were eating like kings but, in all truth, we weren't. It was mostly bits of fish and crabs and fruit and veg. I could see people's minds slipping as they struggled to stay in the game. By the time we reached Restoration Island I was struggling even to get up a tree and grab a few coconuts. But at least the island lived up to its name.

We met its only occupant, long-bearded David Glasheen, an ex-stock market millionaire who'd been there for twenty years, having lost millions in a financial crash. Although he was forbidden from giving us food, he did let us have a nice drink of rainwater. We fished off the boat for sustenance and

I managed to bury an axe in my foot, all the way to the bone, while chopping wood. Luke stitched me up, three in the foot and one in the shin. All I had to do was prevent it getting infected. That meant keeping it dry at all times, which was not going to be easy. But at least, with Ben and Chris now history, the last two weeks and 1,400 miles of the voyage should be free of negativity and politics.

Well, that's what I thought. As we were leaving Restoration Island, I asked Conrad to hoist the sails and get moving, and told a couple of the other lads to put all the pots and pans away. But to my surprise, Conrad refused.

'Let's put the pots and pans away first,' he said, 'then I'll sail. I can't sail like this.'

'I'm just asking for a bit of concurrent activity, that's all,' I said. 'It's not a drama. Get the sails up.'

'How am I meant to sail …?'

'Conrad, listen to what I'm saying!'

Something was up with him. After thousands of miles of team-playing and camaraderie, he was suddenly trying to assert his authority. This was the prickly, domineering Conrad I'd met all those months ago at the London club. While the other lads seemed to have recovered from their mental exhaustion at Restoration Island, he hadn't. As we broke the back of this final push towards Timor, he started making rash and snappy decisions. Soon, I began to suspect there was more to it than simple ratty, dizzy tiredness. Now he'd had the chance to observe me leading the crew for a time, he thought he knew how it worked and that he could do it himself. I was suspicious, too, that now we were nearing the end, he thought he was running out of time to be shown on television as the big alpha male.

A couple of days later we arrived for a brief layover at Sunday Island. There was nothing on there, and we'd only landed because Bligh had done so, and *he'd* only landed because he was an explorer and he wanted to put his flag on it. I had a walk to look for water, but there were only trees and rocks. It was a useless, barren lump. I decided we'd stay the night and rest up before embarking on the final stretch to reach home. That evening, as the sun set, I noticed Conrad was isolating himself, sitting far away on his own, not talking to anyone. You could feel an edge of hostility around him, burning like a rim of fizzing acid. He was making people uncomfortable.

We were five hundred miles out of Timor when the wind stopped completely and the sun became so hot it started melting the batteries in the cameras. Much of the water we had on board had become undrinkable. It had taken on the smell of rotten eggs, and those who tried to swallow through the foul taste ended up firing liquid shit into the glassy millpond of the ocean. I had to reduce our daily ration to just six hundred millilitres.

There wasn't a ripple on the sea or a breath of wind in the sails now. The sky was empty but for the streaky traces of high, pale cloud. We were stuck, and we dried out like husks.

There was nothing to see but the contour of the earth. It was as if we weren't in the real world anymore, but were a speck of dust lost in an alien dimension of blue. It looked like heaven and it felt like hell. Slowly, people started to unravel. The temperature soared through the forties and hit the early fifties. Freddy's resting heart rate fell from sixty to thirty. And Conrad started getting distinctly twitchy.

'I think we should row,' he said out of nowhere one day. This was insanity. Shakingly, I pulled my sweating body out of my place in the shade of a sagging sail. There are few things more dangerous on earth, I've learned, than a man who's lost his mind but believes he's thinking straight.

'Conrad,' I said, 'We're five hundred miles out. We can't row.'

'We should row,' he said. 'Get out of this patch of weather.'

'The men are going down as it is. We're seriously dehydrated. We're on three hundred and fifty calories a day. If we row for just an hour, that's six hundred calories. We're going to put people at serious risk. And for what? We'll cover two or three miles.'

I can understand the urge to do something when you're in trouble. But you should never underestimate the power of intelligent waiting.

The following morning I opened my eyes to see we were still marooned deep in the doldrums. It soon became apparent that, as I'd slept, Conrad had gone round the lads, persuading them that we should indulge his madness. I had to nip this attempt at undermining me in the bud. I called all hands on deck. The men before me were dazed and fading, nothing but ribs and dry, drooping eyes, their clothes hanging off hips and shoulders like rags.

'Guys, we've got one row left in us,' I said. 'If we get fifty miles away from Timor, that will be our last row. So this is what we're going to do. We'll put it to a vote. If this vote goes against me, I will step down and let Conrad captain this boat. Who wants to row?'

Nobody put their hands up.

After five or six days of drifting we finally hit the Timor current. A few days after that, for the first time in ten days, the wind picked up. We were on our way. But our unplanned trip to the doldrums had left us dangerously low on water. Freddy was clearly losing his grip and had become so bad that we allowed a member of the medical team on board to check him over. After carrying out urine tests on all of us, he told us that had we been in England we'd all be on a drip. Our risk of chronic dehydration was such that we were in danger of giving ourselves permanent liver damage. He was putting enormous pressure on me to allow fresh water on board, but most of the lads refused.

It was incredible to see. They were willing to suffer serious health issues for the rest of their lives – and go without proper water for the next four or five days – just to get this job done as authentically as possible. I was proud of them. It had been my intention to create a bubble of us against the world, with no outside influences creeping in. When that bubble is there, everyone comes together, the mission takes over and you all combine into one connected unit. It's a kind of magic.

After sleeping on it, I decided that we'd gone far enough. I had to remind myself that, outside the bubble, this was just a TV show. I couldn't live with myself if Freddy or Luke or Rish, or anyone, ended up in a wheelchair for the rest of their lives because of an act of stubbornness on my part. I permitted everyone to drink as much as they could for twelve hours. Then, when we were fully rehydrated, we were strong enough to row. Everyone did an hour on and an hour off. Within twenty miles we hit the current. It carried us twenty miles further in. We rowed and rowed, all through the night, then in the morning Conrad spotted land. The rest is a blur. I remember anchoring up, wading in and collapsing on a bed of still, white pebbles. I remember joy. I remember gratitude. I remember the burden of leadership lifting off my shoulders, and the sheer release bringing me to tears.

As soon as I pulled myself back together, I grabbed an iPhone from a member of the production crew. Handling such a modern piece of technology, for the first time in sixty days, I felt amazed. You could just click this button and look what it did! I was like a monkey seeing fire for the first time, completely blown away by it. On the day I'd left for Tonga, Emilie had been seven months pregnant. I'd been present for the births of all of my children. I was hoping against hope that I wouldn't miss this one. I dialled shakily. She picked up after three rings.

'It's my due date today,' she said. 'It's not happened yet. How soon can you get here?'

I left on the first flight home. I was by her side, in Broomfield Hospital in Chelmsford, to witness the birth of my youngest son. We named him Bligh.

A few days after my arrival back in London I got a text from Rob Coldstream at Channel 4, the executive who'd been so curious to see if I could talk the talk.

'Congratulations!' it said. 'I hear it was amazing.'

I texted straight back.

'Told you I'd deliver,' I said. 'Next time, can you get me something a bit more challenging?'

LEADERSHIP LESSONS

Winning battles is often about timing. Yes, you should choose your battles, as the old adage goes, but you should also choose when to fight them. My battle against health and safety ruining the authenticity of the voyage was fought at the right moments, and that's how I managed to win.

Give people a chance. Then give them another. Then give them another still. But if they refuse to learn, as Chris did, the only place for them is the gangplank.

Keep your doubts to yourself. Especially in times of pressure, the most important thing a team requires of its leader is certainty. Through a lot of the voyage I was a mess of doubts. I had to live with them and cope with them alone. If I'd shown any cracks, I'd have probably had a mutiny on my hands, just like my predecessor Bligh.

Don't lose sleep if people don't respect you straight away. And don't take it personally. It's human nature. I guarantee that life will offer you the opportunity to prove why you're the leader. And when it does, it's all up to you.

THE ULTIMATE
LEADERSHIP LESSON

BY NOW, I hope you can believe me when I say that I've lived many lifetimes in my thirty-seven years. I've fought many battles and dodged many deaths. I've pushed myself up peaks and down troughs that have broken many of those around me. I consider that, by now, I've earned the right to call myself a leader.

But from that straightforward statement follows a straightforward question: what makes a leader – nature or nurture? Are they born or are they made? The experiences of my life convince me that leaders are made. They're moulded in the fire that naturally burns when impossible situations meet relentless individuals. If you tackle enough problems, and tackle them well, then you too will inevitably become a leader.

Over the pages of this book I've described many of the lessons I've learned along the way: don't let other people define you; don't allow mistakes to win; use your enemy as an energy, and so on. But there's one deeper principle that underpins every single one of them. It's the ultimate leadership lesson, the holy truth that powers them all. Positivity.

No matter how much trouble I've managed to get myself in, the only way I've ever got myself out of it is by keeping a positive mindset. In my darkest moments, when sheer panic and despair felt as if they were closing in, I've always made sure that I've taken a moment to stop and think, 'This is actually happening. I'm in this moment, and it is a negative one. And if I think negatively in a negative situation, then this is only going to go one way.'

If positivity is the secret principle of success, then negativity is its opposite. Negativity is a poison, and I've known my fair share of people who've drunk deeply of that particular toxin. They're the ones who accept all the credit and deflect all the blame. If they manage to become leaders – and sometimes they do – they usually fail. They're the leaders who, because they're not honest about their own mistakes, breed contempt in their subordinates. Rather than admit their flaws and points of confusion, they deny them and blame everyone else when things go wrong. Nobody wants to help them. Nobody has their back. They become isolated and bitter.

People can't trust leaders like this because if they're lying to themselves, they're going to be lying to other people too. It's clear that such leaders' view of the world is distorted. Their number one priority is not leading the team towards its objective but defending themselves. That's the kind of mindset that breeds selfishness and self-obsession. In a military setting, it ends with the bodies of brave young men lying dead on the battlefield.

I've come to believe that the only cure for this poison is a positive mindset. It recasts life's most difficult problems as challenges. Prison was a prime example for me. The instant the judge sentenced me, I took it as if he'd personally challenged me. I decided I was going to be the best inmate in there. Even at my lowest points, I was always trying to be the best. By doing so, those negatives magically turned into positives.

You might now be wondering, how do I foster a positive mindset? How do I become the kind of person who can experience something as bleak as a prison sentence, not as a disaster, but as a challenge? And, more than that, how do I become the kind of leader that people want to follow?

There are three steps to achieving a positive mindset. I'm not calling them 'three easy steps' because they're not easy – but they're infinitely possible. You don't have to be a special person to do them, but you do need courage. The first step is the hardest. In fact, it might even be the hardest thing you do in your life. You should stand in front of the mirror and be brutally honest with yourself. You won't want to be. Every atom in your body may well resist. Criticism from other people is bad enough – the last thing you need is criticism from yourself.

But I want you to rip yourself to bits. Look yourself in the eye and say, 'What don't I like about myself?' It doesn't matter if it's something physical or something to do with your personality or character. You know what those things are. Perhaps you're annoying. Or big-headed. Or talk too much. Or you're patronising. Or you're a nightmare when you're drunk. Name the things you need to change about yourself. Look yourself in the eye and say them out loud, every single one. And don't hold back. This is about brutal honesty.

The moment you can achieve this level of honesty is the moment you can start accepting yourself for who you are and make those changes to become a better you. This level of honesty frees you. It also bulletproofs you against the criticism of everyone you'll ever meet.

Step two. Blame yourself. I don't care how many reasons you have for blaming other people or events from your past. Maybe your mother beat you. Maybe your father left home. Maybe you're not as clever as you might want to be. Maybe you're poor. Maybe you suffer from depression. Maybe you had polio and walk with a limp. I promise you, there's not a man or woman on earth who can't list a host of reasons that lie behind their failures. And guess what? They're right. In reality there are usually multiple reasons for failure, and many of those reasons will be out of our control.

But I don't care about any of that – and neither should you. Looking backwards will not take you forwards. So let's say it's true that some of your problems today have their roots in something that happened twenty years ago. What are you going to do about that, assuming you haven't got a Tardis parked in your back garden? This kind of blameful, backwards thinking is a dead end. It will only lead to you feeling like a victim. It will demotivate you. It will leave you angry and resentful. It will take up valuable headspace. It will exhaust you.

Even if you're completely convinced that all of your problems are someone else's fault, find a reason why they're your fault. Again, look yourself in the eye and say it out loud. Be relentless. Rip into yourself. By accepting and believing that you're responsible for your life, you'll find a way to process your weaknesses, accept them and move on. You'll make progress, sometimes rapidly and dramatically.

Step three. Fix yourself. Stop doing those things you've identified as flaws. If you're annoying when you drink too much, drink less. If you're patronising or big-headed or talk too much, watch like a hawk for those behaviours. You won't wipe them out immediately. Sometimes you'll take three or four steps back. But see every step back as a new challenge to tackle. Keep focused on how much better your life will be when you've finally fixed those problems that have been grinding on you for so many years.

If you tackle this final step in a positive way, then you'll soon start seeing real benefits. It starts with honesty because, as soon as you're honest with yourself, you'll stop fearing what other people think about you. You'll be less afraid of criticism because you'll have done all the criticising yourself.

People might think I'm an arrogant twat, but that doesn't bother me because I've looked in the mirror and I know that I'm not. The people that do think like that don't know me.

Once you stop worrying about what's in other people's heads, you'll stop desperately trying to please them. You'll cease being the kind of person who's running around like a puppy, trying to charm everyone into submission. Confidence will start to emanate from you like light from the sun, and it won't be that horrible, chippy confidence that demands respect. It will be the true, positive, charismatic confidence that radiates from people who know themselves in all their glory and ugliness, and have accepted themselves as what they are.

Soon you'll find improvements in most, if not all, areas of your life. Your relationships will improve, at home and at work. If you've spent your life blaming your boss, your partner or your father for all your shortcomings, you've been making your relationships work against you. Once this process is thrown into reverse, everyone's going to like you more. They're going to want to be closer to you, to work with you, to help you, and will cheer when you succeed.

The entire world will start to look brighter. You'll have more mental energy. You'll become smarter. Why? Because negativity is an obsessive distraction. You can only focus properly on one thing at a time, and negative people are often constantly preoccupied by thinking about all other people they resent and blame. This is how negative people do problem solving – they solve the problem of how bad they feel about themselves by projecting it outwards. Once you've gone positive, that same mental capacity is employed with solving the actual problem!

Your social world will also become transformed. We act our thoughts. If you fill your mind with hate, you'll become a hateful person and you'll therefore attract hate towards you. Turn it around and you'll start drawing people in. When you're brutally honest with yourself it allows you to be brutally honest with others. That doesn't mean being disrespectful and shaming people, but it does mean being unafraid to identify people's weak spots and voice them honestly and openly.

That's the essence of good leadership. With your newfound positive charisma, more often than not, people will react positively and ask for help. Before you know it, people will begin to think of you as a leader. And then the most magic thing of all happens. You realise that they're right. You *have* become that leader. You've turned into the person you always knew, deep down, you could be. The kind of individual who always wants to be first man in.

ACKNOWLEDGEMENTS

AS YOU CAN tell from what you've just read, my life has had its fair share of ups and downs. Along the way, and through each challenge, there have been people who stood by me and helped me become the man I am today: my uncle Andy, Julia and Philip, my mother- and father-in-law, Mike Morris and my older brother Michael. And of course, my wife Emilie and my beautiful children, Oakley, Shyla, Gabriel, Priseïs and Bligh. Without you guys, none of this would ever have been possible. I love you all so much.